John Major

111 Places
in Brooklyn
That You Must
Not Miss

Photographs by Ed Lefkowicz

111 Places in Brooklyn
John Major

emons:

To Frances and Charles Major,
who gave me roots and wings

© Emons Verlag GmbH
All rights reserved
Photographs by Ed Lefkowicz, except:
Butter and Scotch (ch. 27): Paul Wagtouicz;
House of Yes (ch. 63): Kenny Rodriguez;
Masstransiscope (ch. 70): Bill Brand;
Niblo's Garden (ch. 78): Karen E. Seiger;
Watertower (ch. 108): Matthew Pugliese
Art Credits: 9/11 Memorial at Pier 69 (ch. 1): Robert Ressler;
Topaz – Frank Kelly Freas Tribute (ch. 17): Topaz
with Poet, Amuze, Jerms, Rise, and Swift;
ESPO's Art World (ch. 44): Stephen "Espo" Powers;
Masstransiscope (ch. 70): Bill Brand; Misses Brooklyn
and Manhattan (ch. 71): Brian Tolle; Pioneer Works (ch. 82):
Maia Cruz Palileo; Pratt Sculpture Garden (ch. 84):
Mihai Popa, "Ecstacy"; Water Tower (ch. 108): Tom Fruin
© Cover motif: Matthew Pugliese (photography);
Tom Fruin (artist)
Layout: Eva Kraskes, based on a design
by Lübbeke | Naumann | Thoben
Edited by Karen E. Seiger
Maps: altancicek.design, www.altancicek.de
Basic cartographical information from Openstreetmap,
© OpenStreetMap-Mitwirkende, ODbL
Printing and binding: Lensing Druck GmbH & Co. KG,
Feldbachacker 16, 44149 Dortmund
Printed in Germany 2018
ISBN 978-3-7408-0380-3
First edition

Did you enjoy it? Do you want more?
Join us in uncovering new places around the world on:
www.111places.com

Foreword

Many years ago, at the opening of an art exhibition at Long Island University's Brooklyn campus, the great Elliot Willensky, author of the indispensable *AIA Guide to New York City* and the official Brooklyn Borough Historian, gave the keynote address. The show comprised paintings of the city, and his topic that evening was befittingly about *palimpsest*, a word I hadn't encountered before. Willensky explained that the word describes "a manuscript that has been erased in order to be reused, but upon which visible traces remain." He then proceeded to apply this framework, suggesting it as a way to gaze upon Brooklyn. All around us, he proposed, were the constructed and lived-in elements of a landscape that began as a natural tabula rasa but which, for several centuries, had been periodically erased, only to be built up and lived in yet again.

I've thought of Willensky's notion often over these past months as I've considered how to capture the breadth and depth of the borough I'd only just begun to encounter back in 1985. With absolute certainty, I can say that I have fallen short. In fact, there is no easy, straightforward way to capture the story of this tract of land first peopled by Lenape, then Dutch, then English, and then immigrant peoples from every corner of the world. Not only that, I had my own complicated lived experience to consider, arriving as a student / tourist only to later live here, move away, then return, abiding here first as a young man, then as a father, and now finding myself with an empty nest. The borough, and my life in it, has been a sheet of paper scribbled on again and again, with words written that I can read at any given moment, but with tiny hints at what came before still peeking out underneath, and hopefully with more to come.

So, here are 111 places that tell at least part of the story of what this place is and has been, of how it was made and who made it. The place I call home.

– JM

111 Places

1 9/11 Memorial at Pier 69

Brooklyn remembers those who were lost

Looking at the Lower Manhattan skyline from Bay Ridge's American Veterans Memorial Pier, it's not difficult for your mind's eye to wander back to that early September day in 2001 when everything about the world seemed to change. Where the 104 stories of the new One World Trade Center stand now, its shiny glass structure looking in certain light like a torch held aloft, were the Twin Towers, first belching dark smoke into a cloudless cerulean sky and then dissolving and disappearing from view. From this spot on Pier 69 many Brooklynites watched the morning of September 11th unfold. Now there stands a memorial.

Cast at a foundry in Greenpoint, *Beacon* is a 25-foot bronze replica of a trumpet of the kind 19th-century fire brigades used to issue warnings to crowds and instructions to the volunteers. Created by Brooklyn artist Robert Ressler, the trumpet stands on end, as if ready to be taken up at a moment's notice so that orders can be given. Around the base, the inscription reads "Brooklyn Remembers… For Those Lost on September 11, 2001." In all, 36 people from Bay Ridge were among the dead. A small light in the sculpture's crown burns each night, keeping their memories alive.

Among Brooklyn's memorials to 9/11 victims are more than a dozen streets renamed for the fallen. A memorial wall at MCU Park at Coney Island (904 Surf Avenue) commemorates 416 first responders – firefighters, NYPD and Port Authority officers – who died on 9/11 and is illuminated every night until 11pm.

Outside FDNY Squad 1 in Park Slope (788 Union Street), a memorial honors the 12 members (of its 27 member team) lost that horrible autumn day. Nicknamed the "One and Only Squad," the house is charged with particularly high-risk responses. Entitled *Out of the Rubble*, the sculpture featuring two firefighters raising a flag was carved from a single Sitka spruce by Nyal Thomas and Rick Boswell.

Address American Veterans Memorial Pier, Bay Ridge Avenue, Brooklyn, NY 11209, www.nycgovparks.org/parks/american-veterans-memorial-pier | Getting there Subway to Bay Ridge Avenue (R) | Hours Unrestricted | Tip During early spring, several Brooklyn parks, including Brooklyn Bridge Park, feature a living 9/11 memorial courtesy of The Daffodil Project. The city-wide project began when a Dutch grower donated half a million bulbs to commemorate the tragic events. To date, more than 6.5 million bulbs have been planted (www.ny4p.org/the-daffodil-project).

2 Abraham Lincoln's Pew

Take a seat with the great emancipator

Located in the heart of beautiful brownstone Brooklyn Heights, Plymouth Church of the Pilgrims is a well-preserved architectural gem. Built in 1849, it is known for its associations with the Underground Railroad, especially through its first minister, Henry Ward Beecher. Brother to novelist Harriet Beecher Stowe, whose *Uncle Tom's Cabin* was so important to the national conversation about slavery that President Lincoln later called her "the little lady who started this great war," Beecher was also greatly interested in social reform, especially abolition. He held mock slave auctions in the church sanctuary to purchase the freedom of slaves and raised money to send rifles (nicknamed by the press as "Beecher's Bibles") to anti-slavery forces in "Bloody Kansas." A secret area of the church basement (which can be visited on a tour of the church) served as a stop on the Underground Railroad as a hideaway for fugitive slaves.

In October 1859, Plymouth's congregation offered Abraham Lincoln, known widely from his debates with Stephen Douglas the previous year as an opponent of slavery, $200 to give a public lecture on the topic. The speech was scheduled for February 27, 1860, but in order to accommodate the huge demand, the event was relocated to Cooper Union's auditorium in Manhattan. Fifteen hundred people heard Lincoln begin his campaign for the presidency, laying out the Republican position: "Let us have faith that right makes might, and in that faith, let us, to the end, dare to do our duty as we understand it."

The day before, Lincoln ferried over to Brooklyn to hear Beecher preach. Tours of Plymouth Church, offered most Sundays after services at 12:30, provide the opportunity to rest in the pew where Lincoln sat that day in Brooklyn. Imagine the galleried sanctuary filled to capacity on that snowy Sunday as the preacher delivered his fiery sermon.

Address 57 Orange Street, Brooklyn, NY 11201, +1 (718)624-4743, www.plymouthchurch.org | Getting there Subway to High Street–Brooklyn Bridge (A, C), Clark Street (2, 3); walk along Henry Street to Orange Street | Hours Regular services Sun 11am; tours Sun 12:30pm | Tip Visit the Brooklyn Historical Society to see a replica of their rare copy of the Emancipation Proclamation (128 Pierrepont Street, Brooklyn, NY 11201, www.brooklynhistory.org).

3 — Acme Smoked Fish Fridays

Whitefish and herring and trout – oh my!

"Many of our customers treat us like family," Acme Smoked Fish's co-CEO Adam Caslow says. "They come to us to buy the fish for their weddings, their bar mitzvahs, their parties, even after they've moved out of the neighborhood." Caslow is the fourth generation to run the business, which modestly began in 1905 when his great-grandfather Harry Brownstein arrived in Brooklyn from Russia and began selling fish he bought from local smokehouses to shops out of a horse-drawn cart. Thirty years later, Harry and a partner formed a smoked fish company in Brownsville. By 1954, Harry and his two sons opened the plant on Gem Street, choosing the name "Acme" not because it was a superlative but because it would be listed first alphabetically.

Primarily a wholesaler, Acme packages and ships smoked fish, fish salads, and spreads to markets and restaurants throughout the US under several product lines. But informed locals know that once a week, Acme opens its doors for a few hours to let the shoppers purchase their smoked salmon, pickled herring, and whitefish salad directly from the source.

Entry into the Friday market comes in the form of a sign board near a door at the factory. Expect to wait a while, which will give you time to ponder your selections from the list of what's available handwritten on chalk signs. It's not unusual to observe the hardworking women and men who process the fish in hair nets and smocks coming and going. Then, it's through to the factory back room, where the treasures are held: boxes of Acme's signature smoked or peppered salmon, salmon jerky, and whiting, as well as jars of herring in wine or cream. But the real prize is the counter of fresh mackerel, sable, trout, whitefish, herring, and salmon, cut to order by knowledgeable Acme staff, who provide expert advice. Bring cash for your purchases, as no credit cards are accepted.

Address 30 Gem Street, Brooklyn, NY 11222, +1 (718)383-8585, www.acmesmokedfish.com | **Getting there** Subway to Nassau Avenue (G); entry to the Friday market is usually marked by a sign board | **Hours** Fri 8am–1pm | **Tip** After your shopping is complete, grab a coffee and a pastry just around the corner at Norman (29 Norman Avenue, Brooklyn, NY 11222, www.restaurantnorman.com). The bright and open warehouse-like design makes it the perfect place to hang out for conversation with friends.

4 __ Artists and Fleas
The heart of handmade and vintage Brooklyn

"One of the things I always suggest is that if there is a product you are really interested in, talk to the merchant who is selling it to you," offers Stephanie Black, market manager and lead curator at Williamsburg's top multi-merchant marketplace, detailing how shoppers can make the most of their experience. "Often they will be the person who actually created the item and who will give you a story and background on the item that you could never imagine. Sometimes that's running their hands over their object to show you where a cut was made or where they sanded it. Other times they will describe the inspiration behind a particular design."

In an era of mass production and volume retail, this is the kind of experience that discriminating shoppers crave: slowing down and taking the time to look, consider, and engage. Founded in 2003 by Amy Abrams and Ronen Glimer as a one-day-a-week pop-up, Artists and Fleas has evolved into a multi-venue agora operating both days every weekend of the year. Located in the combined space of two old neighborhood warehouses, the market works overtime to maintain an edgy, funky vibe. "We pride ourselves on discovery," Black adds, noting the market supports all manner of designers and makers, from handcrafted jewelry designers and T-shirt silk screeners, to vendors producing hypoallergenic bath and body goods. "With small designers, you can find that cutting-edge product that they test drive along with their greatest hits."

Vendors fully reflect the diversity of Brooklyn, and Black notes with pleasure how all that history and experience is present each market day. With between six to ten thousand visitors each weekend, shoppers may wish to strategize about the kind of experience they prefer. "Saturday is fun for the spectacle, but it's more crowded," Black says. "Sundays at lunchtime tend to be when merchants can take a bit more time."

Address 70 North 7th Street, Brooklyn, NY 11249, +1 (917)488-4203, www.artistsandfleas.com | **Getting there** Subway to Bedford Avenue (L) | **Hours** Sat & Sun 10am–7pm | **Tip** Smorgasburg is one of the most exciting places in the city for people who love food. It's a weekly food market featuring 100+ local food vendors. The venues change seasonally, but you will always find unique international fare that will broaden your palate and keep you coming back for more (www.smorgasburg.com).

5_Balady Halal Foods
The market that provides a taste of home

For the last dozen years, this Bay Ridge grocer specializing in halal foods has offered a feast to the community. Following Islamic religious traditions to fast throughout the day during the month of Ramadan, Balady Market's feast is laid out on tables along the street after sunset, offering food to employees, neighbors, and passersby, Muslims and non-Muslims alike. The ritual, called an *iftar*, is consistent with the principles of Islam about giving and, typically, several hundred hungry people from the neighborhood take part, devouring lamb, chicken, and *kifta* (a Middle Eastern meat patty) augmented with rice.

Balady is an Arabic word that roughly means "my country" or "native." With imported items from throughout the Middle East, then, this is where Bay Ridge's Middle Eastern community shop for the regional flavors and qualities of home. An important component of that is *halal*, the standards for food preparation and consumption laid out in the Qur'an. Muslims are instructed to eat healthfully and nutritiously so as to contribute their best to Islam. This means not consuming forbidden (*haram*) items and making certain, for example, that meat is slaughtered according to prescribed rituals that include prayer. Balady makes certain that all of their goods meet these standards, including having a halal butcher in-house to provide the kind of products their customers seek.

You'll find an olive station with more than a dozen varieties, shelves full of canned goods from throughout the Levant, specialty cheeses and comforting desserts, like halva and baklava. There are tiered islands of lush, colorful fruit and melons, as well as dates galore. Spices for your next *tagine* are in plentiful supply, along with mortars and pestles to grind them, and even hand-painted *tagines* themselves. A beautiful selection of teas are available too, many from the Middle Eastern region.

Address 7128 5th Avenue, Brooklyn, NY 11209, +1 (718)567-2252, www.facebook.com/baladyfoods | **Getting there** Subway to Bay Ridge Avenue (R) | **Hours** Daily 8am–10pm | **Tip** "Muslims in Brooklyn" is a public history project at the Brooklyn Historical Society (128 Pierrepont Street, Brooklyn, NY 11201, www.brooklynhistory.org) celebrating the long and important history of the Muslim community in the borough.

6 Barbès

A South Slope bar that nurtures community

One night it might be a beat-driven Balkan brass band accented by accordian or clarinet playing free-wheeling Macedonian folk or pieces from a Duke Ellington suite, the next night it could be a percussion ensemble performing polyrhythmic improvisation as accompaniment to a reading of Jon Krakauer's account of Himalayan disaster. If it's world music, experimentation, and fun you're after, stop by Barbès in the South Slope for live music seven nights a week.

Named for a north Parisian neighborhood known for its North African population and the music scene that sprouted there in the 1980s, Barbès celebrates the different, the marginal, the unique. Shared appreciation of those qualities also can serve as building blocks for community. It certainly unleashes energy. The intimate performance space and reasonable cover charge means patrons feel connected to the experience in ways that break down arbitrary boundaries, turning strangers into neighbors over time. Grab a beer or a cocktail and a seat in the back, and it won't be long before you might feel like you're at the best house party you've ever attended and watching the band play in an overgrown front room. During the break or after, you might even chat or have a drink with the band members at the bar out front.

A 2017 crowdfunding campaign demonstrated the prudence of this approach. Raising enough money to put Barbès on secure footing for the next five years insures that conversations at this much-needed meeting place for the neighborhood's vibrant artistic community will continue late into the night.

And by the way, those conversations probably aren't hurt by Barbès' collection of single malt whisky, including many 10-, 15- and even 20-plus-year varieties from small Scottish distilleries, along with a dozen beers on tap and a healthy selection of bourbons and tequilas. Relax, enjoy, and make new friends.

Address 376 9th Street, Park Slope, Brooklyn, NY 11215, +1 (347)422-0248, www.barbesbrooklyn.com, barbes@earthlink.net | Getting there Subway to 7 Avenue (F) or to 4 Avenue–9 Street (F, G, R) | Hours Mon–Thu 5pm–2am, Fri & Sat 2pm–4am, Sun 2pm–2am | Tip LunÁtico (486 Halsey Street, Brooklyn, NY 11233, www.barlunatico.com) might be Bed-Stuy's best bar, but it is so much more than that: restaurant, cocktail lounge, music club, late night hangout, and the place for weekend brunch.

7 Bargemusic

Drift away on the music

A floating concert venue situated near the base of the Brooklyn Bridge at Fulton Ferry Landing, Bargemusic offers a sophisticated date night destination for both admirers and casual listeners of classical music. In 1976, Olga Bloom, in the process of retiring from a career as a concert violinist and violist, procured and repurposed a barge that hauled sacks of coffee in New York harbor for most of a century. Reclaimed as a venue offering conservatory students the regular opportunity to perform in public, Bargemusic now offers an ambitious calendar of more than 200 concerts annually.

Concerts mostly consist of chamber music, with a focus on American composers, and are held on a tiny stage in the hull, the performers framed by a triptych of windows looking out over the East River toward the iconic towering structures of Lower Manhattan. Since 2005, Bargemusic has been fronted by Mark Peskanov, an award-winning violinist who has performed alongside music legends Yo-Yo Ma, Isaac Stern, and Midori. Peskanov curated more than 3,000 recitals at Bargemusic, including a series of free concerts for families, "Music in Motion," with unreserved seating, that last an hour and include a Q&A with the musicians.

For the full romantic impact, after the concert, stroll along the waterfront at Pier 1 in Brooklyn Bridge Park, pausing to sit on the stone steps of Granite Prospect, which offers one of the borough's finest vistas for the radiant sunsets that often color the sky behind the Statue of Liberty. The Harbor View Lawn makes a fine spot for a blanket and picnic.

Alternatively, move on to dinner at the River Café or one of DUMBO's other fashionable eateries. Complete your visit by wandering through the warren of narrow cobblestone streets between the Brooklyn and Manhattan Bridges, taking in the swank boutiques to be found along the way.

Address Brooklyn Bridge Boulevard, Brooklyn, NY 11201, +1 (718)624-4924, www.bargemusic.org, info@bargemusic.org | Getting there Subway to High Street–Brooklyn Bridge (A, C) | Hours See website for the concert schedule | Tip Steps away, just beyond the Brooklyn Bridge, is St. Ann's Warehouse (45 Water Street, Brooklyn, NY 11201, www.stannswarehouse.org), an avant-garde performance institution founded in 1980. A 700-seat theater situated within the historic Tobacco Warehouse, St. Ann's Warehouse hosts an annual slate of theatrical and musical events with companies from around the globe.

8__Basil Pizza and Wine Bar

Certified kosher and delicious

Stylish. Creative. Appetizing. Kosher? Though you might be tempted to ask which one of these adjectives does not belong, this chic Crown Heights eatery checks all the boxes. Opened in 2011, Basil Pizza and Wine Bar offers more than just great pizza, tasty though it is. Baked in a gorgeous, state-of-the-art, stainless steel hearth oven capable of burning on both wood and gas, Basil's pizza crust somehow manages to find the sweet spot between crispy and chewy. A number of original options – all vegetarian in order to conform to the laws of kosher and presented with a designer's sense of panache – mean that what makes it to your table feels artistic and imaginative, a fresh take on what may seem like familiar terrain. The Kale and Fire pizza pairs mozzarella and cheddar with garlic confit and habanero peppers, while the Wild Mushroom couples a mozzarella goat-cheese with creminis and shitake mushrooms for a hearty but creamy blend. Fish burgers, smoked salmon sandwiches, and cheese bourekas – all served up with a small salad or basil fries – provide tasty finger-food alternatives.

Basil serves breakfast everyday except Shabbat, offering more standard fare, like eggs Benedict and frittatas, alongside its own singular takes, in the form of Smoked Trout Hash or Latke Rancheros, the latter made with sweet and spicy black bean queso and salsa. A Green Shakshuka combines swiss chard, spinach and fresh herbs with feta, bechamel, and eggs, producing the essence of a dish whose name derives from the Arabic word for "blend."

That blend is also apparent in Basil's patrons. Positioned amidst a diverse thriving neighborhood whose history can too often be reduced to an early 1990s' incident of racial tension, Basil's owners reside in the area themselves, making this a place where the common ingredients are an appreciation of fine food and of the place where they live.

Address 270 Kingston Avenue, Brooklyn, NY 11213, +1 (718)285-8777, www.basilny.com, info@basilny.com | **Getting there** Subway to Kingston Avenue (2, 3, 4, 5) | **Hours** Sun–Thu 8am–midnight, Fri 8am–3:30pm, Sat two hours after Shabbat–2am | **Tip** After breakfast, brunch, or lunch, wander through the "nabe" up to Breukelen Coffee House (764A Franklin Avenue, Brooklyn, NY 11238, www.breukelencoffeehouse.com) for a cup of joe and a pastry. Brewing Red Hook's Stumptown roasted beans, this is the perfect place to read the paper or catch up with friends.

9 Beaux-Arts Court

Serenity now in the Brooklyn Museum

Need a place for quiet reflection or to escape the exhausting pace of hectic city life? One of the most serene spots in all of New York City can be found in the heart of the Brooklyn Museum. At 10,000 square feet, the Beaux-Arts Court on the third floor has the feel of a giant, largely silent *piazza*, framed by a series of classical arches in white. The room is beautifully lit through skylights a full 60 feet above. The laminated glass floor, part of a 2007 renovation effort, seems luminescent as it sits above the original flooring made of handset marble mosaic tiles and pre-cast terrazzo underneath, completed in 1927. Suspended between the two is a brass chandelier. The original design of the museum, executed by legendary architects McKim, Mead & White, called for four such courts. Only this one was completed after plans were dramatically scaled back in a compromise with city government.

Along the walls are paintings and altar pieces from the European art collection, including works by Monet and Breton, and sculptures from the museum's large collection of Rodin. All these works are worthy of longer scrutiny. Research says the average length of time spent viewing a painting is about 15 seconds, but you can take all the time you need. Typically, movable chairs are scattered about, making it easy to pull one up in front of a work that catches your fancy for a longer look.

When you're rested and restored, don't miss the opportunity to take in some of the museum's other treasures. Up on the fourth floor, pause for a gaze down onto the Court before heading to see *The Dinner Party*, Judy Chicago's iconic work celebrating women's history that forms the centerpiece of the Elizabeth A. Sackler Center for Feminist Art. You might also want to take in some of the Egyptian Galleries, as Brooklyn Museum boasts one of the largest collections in the United States.

Address 200 Eastern Parkway, Brooklyn, NY 11238, +1 (718)638-5000, www.brooklynmuseum.org, information@brooklynmuseum.org | Getting there Subway to Eastern Parkway–Brooklyn Museum (2, 3) | Hours Wed, Fri, Sat, Sun 11am–6pm, Thu 11am–10pm | Tip Wander out to the museum's parking lot to see a 47-foot-tall replica of the Statue of Liberty. Originally created to sit atop the Liberty Warehouse of auctioneer William H. Flattau, where it was installed in 1902, the sculpture was donated to the museum a century later.

10__Bed-Stuy on a Bike

Explore this historic neighborhood on the move

Perhaps Einstein had it right when he wrote to his son that life resembles riding a bike, observing "Only when moving can you comfortably maintain your balance." Seasoned urban dwellers know that two wheels trump four. These days, courtesy of the 12,000 bicycles available to share through the CitiBike program, surveying the cityscape is more accessible than ever.

For those who feel like striking out on their own, here are a few highlights to incorporate into an excursion around historic Bed-Stuy. Originally farmland, Bedford-Stuyvesant had its beginning in the Dutch settlement of Brooklyn during the 17th century, remaining largely rural until the mid-19th century. That first changed with the development of the Weeksville community (see ch. 109), then as a middle-class quarter, home primarily to German, Dutch, and Jewish immigrants. Luxurious apartment buildings, such as the Alhambra (500-518 Nostrand Avenue) and the Renaissance (480 Nostrand Avenue), reflect this prosperous moment. Both were designed by prominent architect Montrose Morris, who designed his own home as a calling card to show off his services. Though that showpiece (234 Hancock Street) burned down in the 1970s, other homes on that block showcase his ornate style.

Don't miss Girls' High School (475 Nostrand Avenue), the oldest surviving building in New York City built as a high school. Completed in 1886, notable alumni of this Victorian Gothic masterpiece include actress Lena Horne, congresswoman Shirley Chisholm, and novelist Betty Smith (*A Tree Grows in Brooklyn*). Meanwhile, at the Romanesque Revivalist Boys High School (832 Marcy Avenue), sportscaster Howard Cosell, composer Aaron Copland, and Dada artist Man Ray walked the halls.

Finally, be sure to pass by 404 Tompkins Avenue, where Rose and Morris Michtom created the Teddy Bear. Their original creation now resides at the Smithsonian.

Address Various, Bedford-Stuyvesant, Brooklyn, NY | **Getting there** Subway to Bedford Avenue–Nostrand Avenue (G) | **Hours** Unrestricted | **Tip** The Bedford-Stuyvesant Restoration Corporation (1368 Fulton Street, Brooklyn, NY 11216, www.restorationplaza.org), the country's first community development corporation when founded in 1967, helped revive the fortunes of this historic neighborhood, including founding the Billie Holiday Theatre at Restoration Plaza.

11 Bellocq Tea Atelier

A purveyor of fine teas offers the world in a cup

Though Brooklyn is the epitome of 21st-century coffee-crazed hipsterdom, with a long historical pedigree to go with it, this fashionable boutique that shares its name with the famed photographer of New Orleans' Storyville neighborhood evokes sumptuous and sophisticated Jazz Age afternoons of tea sipped on velvety sofas in rooms colored by dappled light. Bellocq Tea Atelier's inconspicuous door along West Street gives nothing away. Inside, visitors are immediately treated to a table display of the full range of teas, impressive for its variation in texture, color, and aroma. Co-founder Heidi Johannsen Stewart has written, "Essentially tea is a journey of water." If so, here is an expedition that conveys us through a host of the finest estates of Asia and Africa each time leaf and water merge.

Beginning life as a pop-up shop along London's tony Kings Road, Bellocq relocated to this side of the pond and has never looked back. Focusing solely on full leaf varieties, Bellocq now features more than 50 pure teas that explore the complete spectrum of the medium, including fermented Chinese *pu-erh* and finely ground Japanese matcha. Bellocq's herbal varieties include a tart hibiscus (apparently a favorite of Cleopatra) and chamomile, both from Egypt, as well as the New World-sourced gems like lemon verbena (origin Paraguay) and mint (origin Oregon).

There's nothing ordinary about even Bellocq's black teas, including an organic Darjeeling with soft floral notes produced on the Makaibari Estate, one of India's oldest, founded in 1859, and Jin Jun Mei, whose fine leaves with fuzzy golden tips from China's Wuji Mountains produce malty notes and a red-amber brew. A line of rare teas includes Da Yu Ling, a Taiwanese oolong grown at high altitude that delivers complexity and character in each sip. A number of unique blends are designed in-house and produced on-site.

Address 104 West Street, Brooklyn, NY 11222, +1 (347)463-9231, www.bellocq.com, inquiries@bellocq.com | **Getting there** Subway to Greenpoint Avenue (G) | **Hours** Wed & Thu noon–6pm, Fri & Sat noon–7pm, Sun noon–5pm | **Tip** Like coffee (see ch. 34), tea has its own illustrious history in Brooklyn. In 1896 The Grand Union Tea Company built the full-block warehouse for their national chain of stores in DUMBO (68 Jay Street, Brooklyn, NY 11201). Now a commercial space, the entry still features the Grand Union logo in the mosaic floor.

12 Better Than Jam

Shoo-be, doo-be, dye

Though the entrance up the stairs is small and unassuming, this creative and clean artist's paradise is nestled among coffee shops and thrift stores. With sewing machines, big tables, drying racks, and full beautiful light, Better Than Jam is a creative, communal space that packs a lot of energy into an ordinary storefront. The ground level is filled with local artists' labors of love. Paper, ceramics and, most notably, textiles (hold for applause) are all attractively displayed for sale and discussion. A friendly and inviting environment, this is the place for 111 intricate "How do they make this stuff?" conversations.

Better Than Jam is the brainchild of Karin Persan, an artist and supporter of local creators, makers, and producers. She not only displays and sells works and goods from fellow artists, but she generously and passionately teaches classes and workshops about media like sewing, screen-printing, and textile dying.

Try a beginner class on Shibori, the traditional technique of dying fabrics with indigo, whose methods remain largely unchanged since the 8th century. Grab a white shirt or dress from a thrift store around the corner or use samples of cotton material to make gorgeous bandana-sized pieces. Using the studio's workspace means not permanently staining the bathtub blue, leaving you with beautiful and unique pieces to bring home.

Sign up using Better Than Jam's easy-to-navigate website, with classes offered at times throughout the day. Prior to class, enrollees will receive an email from Karin providing instructions about what to wear, how to get there, and what you'll need. Group classes are a fun way to hang with friends and stretch some creative muscles. There are intermediate classes and space rental options are available as well. Better Than Jam is truly a mecca for people who long to create and aren't afraid to get a little messy in the process. Dig in!

Address 20 Grattan Street, Brooklyn, NY 11206, +1 (929)441-9596, www.squareup.com/market/better-than-jam-online | **Getting there** Subway to Morgan Avenue (L) | **Hours** Thu–Sun 1–7pm | **Tip** Free Tours By Foot offers just that – free walking tours of Bushwick's graffiti art. Check the website for the schedule (www.freetoursbyfoot.com/new-york-graffiti-street-art-tours/#brooklyn).

13_Biggie Smalls' Brooklyn

Walk the streets of the legendary recording artist

For Glenn Gamboa, pop music writer for *Newsday*, Brooklyn is central to the work of Biggie Smalls. "One of the first things I did when I moved to Brooklyn was go to Biggie's house," he says, "because I really wanted to see where he came from. He and Jay-Z, they really did transform not just hip-hop, but pop music. It took a whole other turn because of them."

Christopher George Lattore Wallace, better known as The Notorious B.I.G. or Biggie, grew up in a late 1980s' Clinton Hill that now, with the arrival of the Barclays Center and bands of gentrifiers, can be difficult to conjure. Gamboa speculates that his music helped fuel those changes. "Biggie helped create this idea of how Brooklyn was cool, even if it was a little dangerous. People moved here to be a part of that."

A number of sites that help tell Biggie's story are clustered around his childhood home – the third-floor apartment at 226 St. James Place where he lived with his mother, Voletta – and offer the chance to glimpse fragments of his all-too-short life. Just around the corner, you'll find Respect for Life (932A Fulton Street), the barbershop he frequented. The Key Food across the street (991 Fulton) was formerly the Met Food Supermarket where he bagged groceries and, later, dealt to make ends meet. Further along, Country House Diner (887 Fulton) was a favorite, where you can still order up the Big Poppa, "a T-bone steak, cheese eggs, and Whelch's grape."

Parties at Orient Temple (197 St. James Place) are where the young Biggie honed the unique elements of his craft. "Before Biggie, hip-hop was still more or less party music and having a good time," Gamboa explains. "The rhymes are fun, everything was happy. Biggie took it and captured the happiness, but he also described his life in a way that people who lived in Akron or all over the country could relate and understand."

Address 226 St. James Place, Brooklyn, NY 11238 (home); see chapter for other addresses | **Getting there** Subway to Clinton–Washington Avenues (A, C) | **Hours** Unrestricted from the outside only | **Tip** Don't miss the superb 38-foot mural of Smalls as King of NY by artists Scott Zimmerman and Maoufal Alouai, at the corner of Bedford Avenue and Quincy Street. Meanwhile, Notoriouss Clothing (514 Atlantic Avenue, Brooklyn, NY 11217, www.notoriouss.com) offers Biggie-inspired clothing at this shop run by the singer's daughter, Tyanna Wallace.

14 Bizarre Bushwick Burlesque

A sexy evening of laugh-out-loud fun

"It took me a few years, but I finally got my tag line," performer Zoe Ziegfeld said from the stage of this intimate club that exudes feisty and ostentatious attitude – in other words, Brooklyn sass. At the mic as "femcee" of the Fuck You Revue's regular gig, Zoe is dressed in only heart-shaped pasties and a g-string, putting both her sizeable snake tattoo and her hirsute bikini line pretty much on full display. Deadpan, Ziegfeld offers, "She puts the 'bush' in Bushwick."

Bizarre Bushwick offers up live entertainment, much of it burlesque, almost every night of the week. Decor evokes a campy horror film – glowing lamps and gaudy chandeliers, several long sofas pushed up against exposed-brick walls, and a long wooden bar with plenty of stools that encourage sidling up to it. A waterfall of shimmering tinsel rains down at the back of the slightly raised stage. A well-conceived brunch and dinner menu, accented by an assortment of signature cocktails, frozen drinks, wines, and beers, make it an easy place to settle into for a show.

"The root of burlesque is farce," notes James Lester, director of *Getting Naked: A Burlesque Story*, a documentary about the genre. "Burlesque sends up powers-that-be, allowing ordinary people to make fun of elites, often expressed through bawdiness." What results, he contends, is a space offering freedom for both performers and the audience: "I see it as this safe utopian space where women and all genders across the spectrum can present and enjoy sexuality and titillation without feeling like it's voyeuristic, exploitative, or dirty."

A combo of risqué humor, drag, dance, striptease, and performance art, there's something for – nearly – everyone. Book a table in advance for a sexy date night or an evening out with friends. Late hours allow you to linger when you don't want the night to end.

Address 12 Jefferson Street, Brooklyn, NY 11206, +1 (347)915-2717, www.bizarrebushwick.com, bizarrereservation@gmail.com | Getting there Subway to Myrtle Avenue (J, M, Z) | Hours Mon–Wed 4pm–4am, Thu 4pm–midnight, Fri–Sun 11–4am | Tip For seaside fun, visit Coney Island USA's "Burlesque at the Beach," offered Friday and most Saturday evenings all summer long. Circus sideshow acts also perform daily during the summer season (1208 Surf Avenue, Brooklyn, NY 11224, www.coneyisland.com).

15 Black Gold Records

Long plays and lattes

"Everybody drinks coffee and listens to records," Jeff Ogiba, co-owner of Black Gold Records, observes. This cozy storefront located along a Carroll Gardens stretch of Court Street simply makes it possible to pursue those two passions simultaneously. "Our idea was to turn a visit to the record store into more of an experience," Ogiba reflects. "We decorated the shop to make it feel cozy and added a coffee shop because we'd be able to open earlier than other record stores and stay open all day."

The result is a first-rate throwback to the best of college campus vinyl shops of the 1980s combined with a coffee house worthy of millenial love. Call the mash-up "long-plays and lattes," perhaps, or "music and macchiatos" – where it becomes possible to begin each morning sipping and savoring a cup of fresh joe to the subtle ticks and cracks of some A-side tunes.

In a world where a few points and clicks can send almost any item you want racing toward your doorstep, there's something refreshing about the serendipity of popping into a record shop and thumbing through the bins. Ogiba and co-owner Mike Polnasek pride themselves on knowing a lot about genres across the board and curating a smart selection for the shop. "Recently, we had this rare Milton Wright boogie record come through the shop. There's just a priceless aspect to walking into a store and being able to learn something or share something with a passionate employee or customer," Ogiba muses. "That's part of why we fight to keep the record store concept alive."

That can mean offering a tiny suggestion to someone who's just starting a collection or trading obscure details with a longtime jazz or blues enthusiast. Priding themselves on fairness, Black Gold also buys collections, meaning their stockpile is always changing. Checking in regularly is part of the old-school mentality they're trying to preserve.

Address 461 Court Street, Brooklyn, NY 11231, +1 (347)227-8227, blackgoldbrooklyn.com, info@blackgoldbrooklyn.com | Getting there Subway to Carroll Street or to Smith–9 Streets (F, G) | Hours Mon–Fri 7am–8pm, Sat 8am–9pm, Sun 8am–7pm | Tip Vinyl enthusiasts are spoiled for choice in Brooklyn. You might also want to check out Human Head Records (168 Johnson Avenue, Brooklyn, NY 11206), Academy Records Annex (85 Oak Street, Brooklyn, NY 11222), or Second Hand Records (1165 Myrtle Avenue, Brooklyn, NY 11206).

16 BLDG 92

Local ships that sailed the world

The area along Brooklyn's East River waterfront can seem to the uninitiated like a drab expanse of warehouses and docks cut off from the rest of the borough. Dubbed Vinegar Hill back in the 19th century, an allusion (in this largely Irish neighborhood) to the Battle of Vinegar Hill that was part of the Irish Rebellion, the area's first commercial shipyards were established just after the Revolutionary War. In 1801, the US government purchased 40 acres and established shipbuilding operations that were central to the Navy for the next 160-plus years.

BLDG 92 offers a gateway to this fascinating history via a free exhibit over three floors in the restored Marine Commandant's House. As you enter the Navy Yard through a pedestrian gate along Flushing Avenue, pause to look at this red-bricked gem originally built in 1857 and designed by Thomas U. Walter, fourth architect of the US Capitol and responsible for the central dome.

A comprehensive timeline on the exhibition's first floor frames the Navy Yard's history against the nation's political and social history. Production here ebbed and flowed alongside the intermittent winds of war, and several craft help tell that story. Though built in nearby Greenpoint, the USS Monitor, the first ironclad steamship built for the Navy fleet, was outiftted and commissioned here in 1862. Built at the Navy Yard, the USS Maine was an armored cruiser commissioned in 1895 but famously sunk during an explosion in Havana Harbor on February 15, 1898. The battleship USS *Arizona*, sunk in the attack on Pearl Harbor, was built in Brooklyn over a 15 month period in 1915–16, as was the USS *Missouri*, built 1941–44, where the treaty to end war with Japan was signed in August 1945.

Don't miss the third-floor displays, which tell the important story of the men and women who worked at the Navy Yard. That spirit of industry and innovation continues today with the 400 businesses now located there.

Address 63 Flushing Avenue, Brooklyn, NY 11205, +1 (718)907-5992, www.bldg92.org, info@bnydc.org | **Getting there** Subway to Clinton–Washington Avenues (G) or to York Street (F) | **Hours** Wed–Sun noon–6pm | **Tip** Sugar substitute Sweet n' Low was introduced just down the street (29 Cumberland Street, Brooklyn, NY 11205) by father and son Benjamin and Marvin Eisenstadt. A mural marks the sweet spot.

17 __ Broadway Junction Graffiti

An outdoor museum of street art that hits the mark

Subway riders who make their way to the octopus-like confluence of lines called Broadway Junction in East New York are in for an artistic treat: one of the most comprehensive graffiti treatments in the city. Exit the station, find Broadway then head west (left), following under the elevated tracks. Walk just a minute or two more to the corner of Conway Street and you will have arrived. On the walls that form the perimeter of a towing company, you'll find a colorful display that is amazing for its creativity and complexity. Featuring work by a number of the medium's best artists, some of which dates from 2013 – 14, these stretches of wall almost seem to explode with energy.

First, head down Conway, where you will find a number of tags, the stylized writing of the artist's name. Among the easier names to decipher is Sebs, an artist from Bushwick who began graffiti at 12 years old. Works by Jerms, Slom, and Rezor are there, the latter's work including not only an angular tangle of letters but also a gorgeous face seen in profile with purple flowing hair. The passage of work spills down the block toward Callahan-Kelly Playground, a park named for two local soldiers who perished in World War I, then continues along Truxton Street.

Coming back to where you began, turn left and continue along Broadway, following another ribbon of the work. Make the turn at Somers Street to see a last section of more expansive wall. This includes, among others, a mural of Martin Luther King, Jr. that combines portraiture, graffiti, and pop-art.

For a look at more contemporary examples of graffiti art, travel to Avenue U, where you'll find works by a pair of international artists on two separate blocks. Along East 27th are pieces featuring a caricatured rat by Italian artist Zedi, while around the corner English artist Phlegm has executed a series of macabre figures.

Address Broadway Junction at Conway Street, Brooklyn, NY 11207 | **Getting there** Subway to Broadway Junction (A, C, J, L, Z) | **Hours** Unrestricted | **Tip** Artists involved in the "DUMBO Walls" project, begun in 2012 and co-sponsored with the NYC Urban Art Program, have utilized a number of spaces created by the BQE as blank canvases, transforming them into venues for public art. The murals celebrate a range of art, including street art and graphic design (various locations, Brooklyn, NY 11201, www.dumbo.is/dumbo-walls).

18 Brooklyn Boulders

Problem-solving that will drive you up the wall

Rock climbing is a sport on the rise, and Gowanus is the place to find folks ready to ascend. Founded in 2009, Brooklyn Boulders is tucked neatly inside a former garage for the *NY Daily News*, their name playfully spray-painted on the building's front. Inside, would-be spider-persons arrive to find friendly staff and a jumble of brightly colored holds bolted above and across a complex matrix of climbing walls that can at times feel like the inside of an origami fold.

The high ceilings and professionally configured rock wall "problems" mean that unique challenges can be set to accommodate each climber's level of skill. Dates, friends, kids, and dedicated climbers easily train in close proximity, even if experience levels are different. Free climbing, as well as with harnessed belays, is available, with safety as the top priority. Friendly and knowledgeable staff are on hand to assist and advise. Small classes allow even novices to the sport to avoid intimidation and instead define their own reasonable achievable goals to strengthen skills.

"Climbing comes naturally to humans, but it really is conditioned out of us," observes Boulder's Alex Heyison. "Kids are better at it. They don't know to be scared, and they don't think there's anything they can't do." Similar to dancing, climbing taps into mobility outside of daily necessity but within the natural repertoire of the human body. Reaching, grasping, or using legs and core strength to hoist the whole body to hook toes onto a hold, then swinging sideways to reach and grip a colored blob on a wall – these movements change how brain connects to body and promote self-confidence.

Before your first visit, visit the Brooklyn Boulders website, click their "first visit" tab, and fill out a waiver in advance. Novices need to be sure to wear comfortable clothes and book an "Intro" class. Shoes and gear are available to rent. Before you know it, you'll be scaling to new heights – one careful step at a time.

Address 575 Degraw Street, Brooklyn, NY 11217, +1 (347)834-9066, www.brooklynboulders.com/gowanus, support@brooklynboulders.com | Getting there Subway to Union Street (R) | Hours Mon–Fri 7am–midnight, Sat & Sun 8am–10pm | Tip If you're looking for another physical challenge, join the kayak polo meet-up at the Brooklyn Bridge Boat House (must be 18+, Pier 2, Brooklyn Bridge Park, Brooklyn, NY 11201, www.bbpboathouse.org).

19 — Brooklyn Cyclones

Bats, balls, and bobbleheads

"For many people, minor league baseball is their first live experience with the game," Billy Harner, Brooklyn Cyclones' director of communications, asserts when asked what the team hopes a fan will come away with after taking in a ball game. "We want our fans to enjoy a fun night out in our beautiful ballpark – to be relaxed and entertained. Especially with kids, we want to help them start a love affair with baseball."

That formula seems to be working. The Cyclones have led the New York-Penn League in attendance every year of their existence. It doesn't hurt that MCU Ballpark, the Cyclones' home, sits on the edge of Coney Island's Luna Park. Or that the Parachute Jump, a remnant of now-defunct Steeplechase Park that some affectionately call Brooklyn's Eiffel Tower, looms just beyond the outfield. Or that the legendary boardwalk alongside the water's edge leads to the stadium. On a moonlit summer night you could be forgiven for feeling this is heaven.

The Cyclones arrived for the 2001 season. The first pro sports team in the borough since the Dodgers left in 1957, fans were hungry for baseball. The team, a single-A franchise for the Mets, promptly sold out that first season two months before it began. Playing a shortened season that runs from mid-June to Labor Day and that comes after Major League Baseball's draft, the Cyclones are often the first stop for baseball's newest talent and count José Reyes, Daniel Murphy, and Scott Kazmir among its alumni.

Part of the off-the-field fun is the team's promotional nights. "For the kids, we've had SpongeBob and Superhero Nights, and there are fireworks after Friday and Saturday games," Harner adds. "Adults enjoy Seinfeld Night, which began in 2014. It's like a Seinfeld convention with a game going on in the background." Becoming the "Sein-clones" for the game, the team has given away Soup Nazi and Jackie Chiles bobbleheads.

Address MCU Park, 1904 Surf Avenue, Brooklyn, NY 11224, +1 (718)372-5596, info@brooklyncyclones.com | Getting there Subway to Coney Island–Stillwell Avenue (D, F, N, Q). Walk along Stillwell Avenue towards the beach, then turn right on Surf Avenue. | Hours See website for game schedules | Tip Before the game, make sure to visit the sculpture of Jackie Robinson and Pee Wee Reese located on the plaza near the park entrance. Created by artist William Behrends and dedicated in 2005, the piece commemorates the friendship between the two Dodger greats that helped promote racial integration in baseball.

20 _ Brooklyn Dodgers Clubhouse

Take me out to the ball game

Located in the heart of Park Slope, the Old Stone House connects to several layers of Brooklyn history. A 1933 WPA reconstruction of the 1699 Vechte family farmhouse incorporating materials from the original Dutch colonial home, the stone house is situated on former farmlands, among the earliest settled by the Dutch. It rests near to what was originally Gowanus Creek, an important early water supply and transportation route. This house played a critical role in the Battle of Brooklyn, the first major combat between American and British troops following the Declaration of Independence – and the largest conflict of the Revolutionary War (see ch. 108).

But few locals know of the Old Stone House's link to early baseball history. In the late 19th century, the Old Stone House was used as the clubhouse to the team later known as the Brooklyn Dodgers. Formed as the Brooklyn Grays in 1883, the team was variously known as the Superbas, Robins, Bridegrooms, even the Trolley Dodgers before exclusively becoming the Dodgers in 1932. Until 1891, the team played games on a field here known, like the playground today, as Washington Park, splitting time at Eastern Park in Brownsville.

Charles Ebbets, who went on to become principal owner of the club, began working for the Dodgers during that 1883 season, selling tickets, peanuts, and scorecards he printed himself. By 1890, Ebbets began investing in the club, owning 80% and becoming club president in 1898. That season, a second, bigger Washington Park opened here, which could seat 15,000 fans, where the Dodgers played for a further 15 seasons. Ebbets began secretly buying parcels of land in part of the nearby Flatbush neighborhood, a former garbage dump known as Pigtown where he wanted to build a larger, more accessible stadium in what became Ebbets Field (see ch. 40).

Address 336 3rd Street, Brooklyn, NY 11215, +1 (718)768-3195, www.theoldstonehouse.org, info@theoldstonehouse.org | Getting there Subway to 4 Avenue–9 Street (F, R) | Hours Fri 3–6pm, Sat & Sun 11am–4pm, or by appointment | Tip Wander across the street to L'Albero dei Gelati (341 5th Avenue, Brooklyn, NY 11215, www.alberodeigelati.com) for some of the finest gourmet Italian gelato in Brooklyn. Founded by three partners from Milan and using fresh local and fair-trade ingredients, unique organic flavors like arugula, rose and rhubarb, and blue cheese attract long lines that are worth the wait.

21 Brooklyn Glass

A furnace glows in Brooklyn

Who knew that a furnace containing twelve hundred pounds of molten glass at a temperature of 2100°F has been burning in Gowanus 24/7 since the summer of 2011? That furnace is the centerpiece of this 10,000-square-foot studio in Gowanus devoted to the ancient art of glassblowing. Offering a five-hour intensive workshop on a Saturday or Sunday for those who want to give it a try or an eight-week course for those who want a more relaxed and sustained approach, Brooklyn Glass has classes for every kind of budding glassblower.

Kat Ablon, who along with David Ablon founded the studio, suggests the practice is surprisingly accessible to all. Small class sizes (usually seven to nine people) gives instructors the opportunity to work closely with individual students. "At first it can be a bit intimidating," she observes. "Sometimes you look at the equipment, and it looks like medieval instruments of torture that were used in the 1300s. But then you start pulling this blob of molten glass, and all at once it turns out to be a beautiful creation." That moment of artistic success can indeed be intense: typically, a beginner's first project will be a flower, Ablon informs, as it involves an opportunity to use the tweezers and get the feel of how to work with molten glass. A glob of material is gathered onto the blowpipe. While working, the pipe is moved in and out of cylindrical openings next to the furnace, called "glory holes," to keep the glass soft and pliable. Once finished, the item goes into the oven – about 900°F – overnight to cool. Other projects include paperweights, highball glasses, or vases. Special classes offer the opportunity to work in neon. Advanced students can work on individual projects, supervised by an instructor. Ablon says, "If you sit at your desk all day long, suddenly you have a sense of, 'Look, I did something that didn't involve tapping on a keyboard!'"

Address 142 13th Street, Brooklyn, NY 11215, +1 (718)569-2110, www.brooklynglass.com, info@brooklynglass.com | Getting there Subway to 4 Avenue–9 Street (F, G, N, R) or to Prospect Avenue (R) | Hours Mon–Fri 10am–9pm | Tip Learn to forge your very own kitchen knife, pie plate, or BBQ tools at She-Weld, which offers classes in blacksmithing, welding, and metalworking (27 Coffey Street, No. 1, Brooklyn, NY 11231, www.she-weld.com).

22 Brooklyn Historical Society

The "walled city" on the waterfront in DUMBO

"Our mission statement calls for us to connect the past to the present to keep Brooklyn's vibrant history meaningful and relevant to the present and for generations to come," Brooklyn Historical Society's Marcia Ely says, when asked to describe its role. "Our mission, on top of our values, is to give voices to those not often heard, to tell the stories that have been buried alongside the stories we've all heard." BHS's new annex in DUMBO, part of the renovation of the historic Empire Stores, does just that, squeezing many different histories of Brooklyn's waterfront into a compact exhibit space.

An eight-minute introductory film sets the stage. Beautiful images allow us to visualize the Native American settlements that existed prior to Henry Hudson's arrival in 1609 and the small settlement in nearby Brooklyn Heights founded in 1646. Development really accelerated in the 19th century, when Brooklyn grew from a tiny outpost with fewer than 6,000 residents to more than a million strong. A large wall map highlights the growth along DUMBO's waterfront, called the "walled city" due to the warehouses that together resembled a fortress.

Small, multi-sensory exhibit stations creatively use pictures, oral histories, and video to highlight stories ranging from women of color who worked during World War II at the nearby Navy Yard to the impact of climate change on the Brooklyn coastline. For young visitors, there's the opportunity to dress up as Rosie the Riveter, make Brooklyn Bridge postcards, or use interactive technology to star in a film about the borough's history. A window display highlights objects found when the Empire Stores site was excavated in the 1970s.

One exhibit uses as a starting point an 1873 obituary of a Michael Harkins at Empire Stores, who died when a sack of feed fell on his head. It's a vivid opportunity to see historians' detective work in action.

Address 55 Water Street, Brooklyn, NY 11201, +1 (718)222-4111, www.brooklynhistory.org/dumbo | Getting there Subway to York Street (F), or to High Street–Brooklyn Bridge (A, C); ferry to DUMBO | Hours Tue–Sun 11am–6pm | Tip The Brooklyn Historical Society's main branch is located in a landmarked Queen Anne-style building (128 Pierrepont Street, Brooklyn, NY 11201, www.brooklynhistory.org). Designed by George Brown Post and opened in 1881, the building is notable for its gorgeous firebrick red terracotta façade. Visit the website for a full schedule of events and exhibitions.

23 Brooklyn Owl

Discover the magic in you

Annie Bruce's life as a unicorn entrepreneur and self-empowerment guru began with a request from her four-year-old daughter Bee. A high school math teacher taking time at home after having children and thinking about what might be next, Bruce recounts, "Bee said, 'I want to be a unicorn.' So, I said, 'Let's figure out how to make you one.'" Soon, heads were turning on Brooklyn streets, and people were asking Bruce and her daughter, "'Hey, where did you get that?' So, I made a bunch of them and started selling them a few weeks later at the Brooklyn Flea," Bruce recounts. "It just took off from there."

That was six years ago. In April 2017, Bruce opened Brooklyn Owl on a Park Slope-adjacent stretch of Flatbush Avenue. Filled with rainbow-colored and sparkling handmade goodies, the shop is a child's enchanted paradise. Unicorn horns (including limited editions like blue or pink mermaid, snow leopard, and Olympic gold), Narwhal horns (in both silver and hot pink sparkle), and softer horns in felt abound. Each comes with a stretchy elastic headband that will allow young unicorns to more fully embody their mythical beast experience. A matching line for adults means mom and dad can join in too.

Bruce believes she's not simply selling a product. "We are telling kids to believe in themselves. We call it 'wearing their magic,'" she says. "They can be more confident, show people who they are and not be afraid to be different." To help, Bruce has created a Unicorn Magical Adventure that customers of all ages can participate in when they visit. Affirmations are hidden throughout the shop that can be repeated into the Magic Mirror. "One mother told me it was better than therapy," Bruce added. Drop-in art project workshops on weekends transform leftover sparkles and materials into creative collages. Horns come in four sizes and many colors, and are all handmade in Brooklyn.

Address 252 Flatbush Avenue, Brooklyn, NY 11217, +1 (718)737-7017,
www.brooklynowl.com, info@brooklynowl.com | Getting there Subway to 7 Avenue
(B, Q), to Bergen Street (2, 3), or to Atlantic Avenue (4, 5, N, R) | Hours Tue–Sat
10am–6pm, Sun 10am–5pm | Tip Visit Pipsqueak Children's Shoppe (1124 Bedford
Avenue, Brooklyn, NY 11216, www.pipsequeakshoppe.com) in Bed-Stuy for more
kid-oriented fun. In addition to a full range of toys and games, the store offers a busy
schedule of activities as well.

24 Brooklyn's Tiny Parks

Good things come in small packages

In a borough that features some of the country's most expensive real estate, it is no surprise that every piece of land should be put to use. That includes park spaces. While Frederick Law Olmstead and Calvert Vaux's Prospect Park, a 526-acre landscaped gem, will always reign supreme, multiple diminutive plots provide important, if less spacious, locations to escape from the hectic pace of city life. Call them Brooklyn's urban planning answer to the tiny house movement.

Several tiny parks honor Brooklyn's fallen warriors. Take Sergeant Joyce Kilmer Triangle, for example (East 12th Street & Kings Highway, Brooklyn, NY 11229). At 1/1000th of an acre (roughly 50 square feet), this tiny plot became a park in 1934 and was named the following year after the well-known poet, who wrote the famous poem, "Trees," loved by legions of school children. Already a renowned poet when he enlisted in WW I, Kilmer was felled by a sniper's bullet at the second Battle of the Marne and was buried in a military cemetery in France.

Fidelity Triangle (601 Meeker Avenue, Brooklyn, NY 11222, www.nycgovparks.org/parks/fidelity-triangle) also commemorates the honored dead of "the war to end all wars." Decidedly more grandiose at 1/200th of an acre, the park, which opened in 1921, features a trio of London planetrees to provide shade and a set of benches to rest upon as you while away the afternoon.

Finally, if you're in Bushwick, take a minute to pause in Freedom Triangle (Bushwick Avenue, Brooklyn, NY 11221, www.nycgovparks.org/parks/freedom-triangle). Formed at the junction of Willoughby, Myrtle, and Bushwick Avenues, the pint-sized park is large enough to accommodate Pietro Montana's sculpture, "Victory With Peace," which features the Greek goddess Nike with an olive branch and a plaque listing the names of the 94 soldiers from the local area who gave their lives in the Great War.

Address Various, see chapter | Getting there See mta.info for subway directions | Hours Unrestricted | Tip A tiny plot found near the intersection of Mackay Place and Narrows Avenue in Bay Ridge may well qualify as the borough's tiniest cemetery. The small burial ground known as the Barkaloo Cemetery (34 Mackay Place, Brooklyn, NY 11209) contains the graves of Harmans Barkaloo and Simon Cortelyou, both of whom served during the Revolutionary War.

25 Bushwick Community Darkroom

Develop your skills and your prints here

The great Diane Arbus, who trained her lens on the marginalized, the outsider, and the unconventional, once made the observation, "Taking pictures is like tiptoeing into the kitchen late at night and stealing Oreo cookies." In other words, the art of the photographer is achieved by stealth, and the result offers a yummy delight.

On that basis, then, Bushwick Community Darkroom is a place to develop both photography and ninja skills, as well as make friends. Begun with just a little equipment and not much money, Lucia Rollow founded BCD in Bushwick in 2011. Having graduated from art school and suddenly without access to a darkroom, she set about to create one for herself and the other folks she was meeting with the same predicament. Putting the emphasis on accessibility and affordability, the studio has grown into a 3,000-square-foot warehouse offering classes and providing an impressive level of access to a comprehensive range of services. Beginners might want to take a four-week "Intro to Black-and-White Photography" course that introduces the camera, film development, and printing from negatives. Classes can be purchased á la carte or as a bundle (which will get you a 25% discount).

From there, it's possible to study more advanced black-and-white or color printing. In fact, the ability to print in color is a somewhat unique capability for a community darkroom due to cost and the limited lifespan of some color prints. BCD also offers the chance to print large-format work, not only standard 35mm to medium format 120mm, but also 4x5 in work. These enlarger capacities are a surprise to find outside of an academic setting.

The darkroom offers very competitive rates for drop-off film development (including E 6), and a membership gets you a healthy credit toward these services.

Address 110 Troutman Street, Brooklyn, NY 11206, +1 (718)218-4023, www.bushwickcommunitydarkroom.com | Getting there Subway to Central Avenue (M) | Hours Mon–Wed 6–9pm, Thu–Sun noon–8pm | Tip Looking to go retro on your photographic adventure? Pay a visit to Brooklyn Film Camera (203 Harrison Place, Brooklyn, NY 11237, www.brooklynfilmcamera.com), offering a full range of Polaroid cameras and supplies, as well as other vintage cameras, to give your snaps the perfect old-school touch.

26__ The Butcher of Hanover

19th-century macabre Berlin comes to Brooklyn

Unsuspecting patrons wandering into what looks like a swanky downtown Brooklyn watering hole can be forgiven if they do a double take. Tucked away in a fourth-floor corner, just beyond the ticket counter of Alamo Drafthouse Cinema, House of Wax's star attractions are the permanent patrons – a museum of death masks and anatomical figures so lifelike that you feel you've stepped through a portal back in time.

Marvel at the mutton chops of Kaiser Wilhelm I, Germany's first emperor. Tudor England's Elizabeth, the "Virgin Queen," is here too, as is Oliver Cromwell, the man who more than a half-century later toppled the throne. Look France's first emperor Napoléon Bonaparte in the face. A fan of music? Keep your eye out for Liszt, Chopin, and Beethoven. The remnants of "Castan's Panopticum," a collection of wax figures that operated in Berlin from 1869 until 1922, the display was so popular in its heyday that it would attract up to 5,000 visitors on a single Sunday afternoon.

Part of the museum's appeal was as a source of "popular science" education. As such, sprinkled in amid the masks of the powerful and famous, you'll find displays showing the effects of diphtheria, a cross-section of tracheotomy surgery, and a woman in the midst of a Caesarian section. Meanwhile, the bar showcases an innovative collection of cocktails, choice wines, and a selection of around 25 microbrew beers on tap.

But, it's probably best to keep your eyes out for Fritz Haarmann. Known as the Butcher of Hanover for having committed at least 24 murders of young men between 1918 and 1924, he lured them to his home under the guise of offering help, only to bite through his victims' Adam's apples.

You'll need a drink after viewing these objects. Try the citrusy Butcher of Hanover or the spicy Napoleon Death Mask cocktails.

Address 445 Albee Square West, 4th floor, Brooklyn, NY 11201, +1 (718)513-2457, www.houseofwax.com, info@thehouseofwax.com | **Getting there** Subway to Dekalb Avenue (B, Q, R) | **Hours** Sun–Thu 4pm–last showing at Alamo Drafthouse Cinema, Fri & Sat 4pm–2am | **Tip** Grab a bite and sit at the long tables in Dekalb Market Hall (445 Albee Square W, Brooklyn, NY 11201, www.dekalbmarkethall.com). From Fletcher's BBQ to Katz's Deli, and from Ample Hills Ice Cream to Steve's Key Lime Pie, more than three dozen vendors showcase their tasty local treats.

27___Butter and Scotch

Every day is your 21st birthday

After a hard week, you've earned the right to sleep late and go off to brunch with friends. If you could imagine the perfect place to meet and eat, what would it be like? Comfort food dominated by savory starches and tasty, filling protein, accented by a touch of something sweet – that's what. And it's all made even better by a meticulously crafted cocktail that can go in one of several directions: fruity and light, like a mimosa; potent posing as healthy, as in a Bloody Mary; or a caffeinated jolt to the system, such as an Irish coffee. Wrap all that up and plop it down in Crown Heights and *voila!* Let the party begin.

Whether it's the Biscuits and Gravy, made just like you wish mama *had* made them, or the BaconEggandCheese, such a delectable blend of flavors that even the name can't bear seeing them separated, this is clearly the way to let yourself know that the weekend has arrived. Totchos add lettuce, diced tomatoes, and queso to tater tots, sprinkling in Hatch green chiles for a bit of spicy zing.

Owners Allison Kave and Keavy Landreth met selling pies and mini-cupcakes respectively at the Brooklyn Flea. They opened this funky drinks-and-dessert venue in 2015, adding a strong dose of "playful" onto the Crown Heights scene. The brightly colored, cozy interior evokes that special place that you'd want to wander into at the end of a good night out. Pull up a stool and drink in the toy figures, lava lamp, and pink plastic pineapple co-mingled with the rows of spirits that crowd the shelves behind the bar. A framed sign at the top coyly reads, "Bitches Love Sprinkles." Butter & Scotch's signature blend of rainbow-colored sprinkles, after all, adorns the crown of pink frosting atop their three-layer Birthday Cake. Meanwhile, the menu lets you know that any pie, cake, or cookie can be blended into a milkshake – a fact which opens the door to possibilities galore. This is a decidedly judgement-free zone!

Address 818 Franklin Avenue, Brooklyn, NY 11225, +1 (347)350-8899, www.butterandscotch.com | Getting there Subway to Franklin Avenue (2, 3, 4, 5), or to Botanic Garden (S) | Hours Mon 5pm–midnight, Tue–Thu 9am–midnight, Fri 9–2am, Sat 10–2am, Sun 10am–midnight | Tip For more tasty Southern fare, make your way to The HotHouse (415 Tompkins Avenue, Brooklyn, NY 11216, www.bcrestaurantgroup.com/ hothouse). Check out the Nashville-style fried chicken, the Low Country Seafood Boils, or Blackened Catfish and Grits for all those authentic touches at this home away from home.

28_ Camperdown Elm

Brooklyn's crowning curio

No more than about 20.5 feet high with a tangle of knotted branches growing more parallel to the ground than upright, the Camperdown Elm would not be a very good place for a treehouse. In fact, it looks more like an oversized bonsai.

Tucked along a sloping embankment near the Boathouse in Prospect Park, this horticultural oddity – almost as old as the park itself – brings a bit of Victorian charm to the middle of the borough. Planted in 1872, the diminutive elm is a rare example of a tree unable to reproduce itself. Discovered by David Taylor, the forester for the Earl of Camperdown in Dundee, Scotland, the original specimen was transplanted to the estate, where cuttings were grafted onto the trunks of other elms. Eventually, those biological duplicates made their way into gardens all over the globe as prized rarities.

Though now a treasured feature of the park, in the 1960s the Camperdown Elm was nearly lost. Long-neglected, the trunk had more than a dozen holes, some plugged with concrete, and the tree became infested with rats and ants. But Pulitzer Prize-winning poet Marianne Moore, a public park enthusiast, penned an ode calling attention to its plight, calling the tree "our crowning curio." The resulting publicity, and a team of experts, helped save the day.

The park features many other captivating spots. The Audubon Center, located in the Boathouse (www.ny.audubon.org/node/6906), features small, hands-on exhibits for both adults and children and offers public programs meant to encourage exploration of Prospect Park's 585 acres. Just steps from the Camperdown Elm is the picturesque Lullwater Bridge with seasonal views that rival Monet canvases. Continue along the path to the Nethermead, the perfect place to enjoy a picnic with friends and family. Early morning walks through the surrounding woods are excellent for bird watching too.

Address Prospect Park, Brooklyn, NY 11225, near the entrance at Lincoln Road and Ocean Avenue, +1 (718)965-8951, www.prospectpark.org, info@prospectpark.org | **Getting there** Enter the park at Lincoln Road and Ocean Avenue. Follow the path into a small tunnel that cuts through an embankment. The Camperdown Elm is just past the tunnel, to the right of the path. | **Hours** Daily 5–1am | **Tip** Visit the nearby LeFrak Center at Lakeside for ice skating, roller skating, and other recreational activities. During summer months, a series of outdoor concerts take place at the Prospect Bandshell.

29 — Caputo's Lard Bread

Old-world bread from an old-school bakery

One Yelp review includes the admonition that if all you care about is healthy eating, then "maybe you should go on with your healthful, sad, lard bread-less existence." So sayeth Peter D., capturing the sentiments of many stalwart fans of this Cobble Hill fixture. This fifth-generation bakery specializing in breads was originally founded in 1904 when father and son Vincenzo and Giuseppe Caputo migrated from Bari, Italy. Crusty on the outside, soft and chewy inside, lard bread is a concoction of zippy pork salami, sharp provolone cheese, and pepper, infused with olive oil. A sandwich in a single loaf, it's pure peasant goodness.

James Caputo, the current baker, assumed the reins of Caputo's 18 years ago. Both of his grandfathers were bakers, and neither wanted him to follow them into the business. "They wanted me to get an education, which I did," he laughs. "For years I was a trader on Wall Street. But I begged my dad to allow me back into the bakery. It was about a three-year battle, but I eventually came out victorious."

Part of Caputo's long-term recipe for continued success is the ability to change with the customers. To survive, the business evolved from a shop that originally made four or five kinds of bread until, now, the full range includes about a hundred different loaves. Even the lard bread is an example of changing with the times. "My great-grandfather baked *ciccioli* bread," Caputo recounts, "made from the renderings of pork fat cooked almost into a paste and put in the bread for flavor. That's no longer in butcher shops, so we had to adapt."

They thrive because, like his forebears, Caputo loves his customers. "They're what get me up every morning," he says, "and many have become friends." Joseph Callari, a customer from Los Angeles, brings home 100 lard breads in a suitcase after every visit for fellow Brooklyn transplants who just can't live without it.

Address 329 Court Street, Brooklyn, NY 11231, +1 (718)875-6871, www.caputosbakery.com | Getting there Subway to Bergen Street or Carroll Street (F, G) | Hours Mon–Sat 6am–7pm, Sun 6am–5:30pm | Tip To satisfy your sweet tooth, make your way to Prospect Heights' Doughnut Plant (245 Flatbush Avenue, Brooklyn, NY 11217, www.doughnutplant.com). With loads of gourmet flavors to sample, these gems (some of which include DP's own handmade jam) are hard to beat – but not to eat.

30__Caucasian Wingnut
A Black Sea immigrant lays down roots

Pterocarya fraxinifolia, the Latin name for the Caucasian wingnut, has none of the comic value of the more common English label for this arboreal rarity. Though conjuring notions of a political extremist, the name of this immense and august tree actually identifies it as a member of the walnut family from the mountainous region between the Black and Caspian Seas where Asia butts up against Europe. The species arrived in Europe in 1782, transported by a French naturalist.

Located just north of the Rock Garden in the area alongside Flatbush Avenue, Brooklyn Botanic Garden's (BBG) own goliath, characterized by its sizeable exposed root mass, is not difficult to find. Arriving from Rome as a sapling in 1922, BBG's example now measures more than 45 feet in height and has a canopy that extends more than 60 feet (propped up on one vulnerable end), while its gnarled and knotty trunk spans 10 full feet in width. Catkins, a drooping flowering strand up to 20 inches in length, appear during the summer. A second tree, propagated from a cutting taken from this first tree, can be found near the Herb Garden.

A short walk away, just south of the Rock Garden, the Mountain Winterberry, a species from the Appalachians considerably closer to home, was one of the 12,000 plants original to the Botanic Garden when it opened in 1911. The nearby Chinese Parasol tree, so named for its large leaves that can grow to 12 inches in width, has been in residence here since 1925, a gift of the Yokohama Nursery in Japan.

For trees of a decidedly more diminutive sort, don't miss the C.V. Starr Bonsai Museum. With over 350 specimens, about 30 of which are on display at any one time, BBG's collection is one of the oldest and largest outside of Japan. One bonsai, a white pine, is more than 300 years old and was brought to Brooklyn from a Japanese mountainside more than 90 years ago.

Address 990 Washington Avenue, Brooklyn, NY 11225, +1 (718)623-7200, www.bbg.org | Getting there Subway to Eastern Parkway–Brooklyn Museum (2, 3) or to Prospect Park (B, Q, S) | Hours See website for summer, winter, and late-night hours | Tip Inspired to do some gardening of your own? Check out Brooklyn Plantology (26 Brooklyn Terminal Market, 1510, Brooklyn, NY 11236, www.brooklynplantology.com) in Canarsie. At 20,000 square feet, this family-owned business offers a wide selection of seasonal outdoor and indoor plants, plus pots and gardening supplies.

31 Cherry Hill Gourmet Market

Russian soul food

The red awning and gold lettering over the entrance on the corner of Emmons Avenue and Ocean Avenue pay homage to Lundy's, the venerable Sheepshead Bay restaurant that began life as a fish market in 1918. Located in the heart of Brooklyn's Russian community on Sheepshead Bay, Cherry Hill Gourmet Market is a destination market that stocks those hard-to-find specialized ingredients that distinguish the gourmet from the ordinary pantry, along with a full range of prepared foods meant to satisfy those homesick for the old country.

The market is set inside a sprawling, stuccoed, Spanish Colonial Revival villa that Frederick Lundy built in 1934 after the city flattened the waterfront side of what was known as the Clam Coast and widened Emmons Avenue. The space was large enough to have served more than 2,500 diners at a time. (During their heyday, Lundy's claimed to serve a million meals a year.) Under the direction of their own chefs working on-site in spacious kitchens, Cherry Hill offers Azerbaijani fare like Baku Salad or eggplant, and Russian favorites like squash caviar, Azu Tartarian style, and beet salad. Red or green borscht, *kharcha* soup, and *okrashka* invoke tasty memories of faraway homelands, 30 years after *Glasnost*.

A well-stocked meat counter houses rows of dried salamis, while there are an ocean of smoked fish options. Shoppers familiar with the cyrillic alphabet will be at an advantage strolling down aisles lined with imported brands supplying kosher and Baltic specialties.

A pick-and-mix display of candies and sweets mimics precisely the experience of fine Eastern European emporiums. Be certain to save some time (and calories!) for Cherry Hill's dessert counter, where artistry of presentation only amplifies the mastery of taste achieved by the market's specialty bakers.

Address 1901 Emmons Avenue, Brooklyn, NY 11235, +1 (718)616-1900, www.cherryhillgourmet.com, contact@cherryhillgourmet.com | Getting there Subway to Sheepshead Bay (B, Q) | Hours Open 24 hours | Tip Walk west along Sheepshead Bay Road to Ocean Avenue, where a pedestrian bridge crosses the actual Sheepshead Bay. Stroll among the mansions of Manhattan Beach. Now home to a large Russian-Jewish immigrant community, the area was originally an upscale resort developed just after the Civil War by Austin Corbin, who, ironically, was a notorious anti-Semite.

32 City Reliquary

From the attic to the museum

The City Reliquary focuses on curios, ephemera, the everyday – the kinds of things that are collected as people's treasures one day, discarded as no longer worth saving the next. City Reliquary began as a series of window displays in the street-level Williamsburg apartment of NYC firefighter Dave Herman, less than a five-minute walk from the current museum's location. Created in the months following 9/11, the display included relics that were intended to heal the community's wounds by evoking memories of the rich, everyday history of the city through tiny, often overlooked fragments of life all around us.

The storefront museum packs a lot of life into its modest-sized set of rooms. Display cabinets filled with ticket stubs, buttons, felt banners, and commemorative teaspoons from the 1939 and 1964 New York World's Fairs sit next to Statue of Liberty figurines in all shapes and sizes and arrangements of subway tokens. Bits of plaster from Grand Central Terminal and the Waldorf Astoria and fragments of mosaic tiles from the employee lounge at TWA's monumental terminal at JFK represent the story of New York's "Geological History," while a wall of Jackie Robinson baseball cards and press clippings celebrates the Dodger legend's significance both on and off the field. A genuine New York newsstand sits in one corner, a barber's chair and tools inhabits another. Even the restroom should not be missed! Sarah Celentano, manager of City Reliquary, describes the collection in archaeological terms: "The items together form a ruin, acquiring new meaning over time." In other words, individual artifacts provide an opportunity for time-travel, becoming the tiny part that evokes the whole, transporting us to another era.

A small outdoor garden serves as a community space for an active calendar of poetry slams, musical performances, and film screenings.

Pause for a moment and breathe in the city around you.

Address 370 Metropolitan Avenue, Brooklyn, NY 11211, +1 (718)782-4842,
www.cityreliquary.org, info@cityreliquary.org | **Getting there** Subway to Metropolitan
Avenue (G) | **Hours** Thu – Sun noon – 6pm | **Tip** Make your way to Cobble Hill's art
project in progress – the Mosaic House (108 Wycoff Street, Brooklyn, NY 11201). In the
wake of 9/11, the home's owner, Susan Gardner, began attaching bits of tile, glass, shells,
and buttons to the façade, transforming her brownstone into an artistic exploration.

33 Cocoa Grinder

A cup of joe with a philosophy of life

There's a lot to love about this Bay Ridge business that owner Abdul Elenani calls "a coffeehouse on steroids." The stylish decor, dominated by clean lines and organic materials, has just the right ratio of smart to casual. Coffees are sourced from small farmers overseas and roasted on-site. An array of fresh-squeezed juices and protein shakes provide a nourishing lift, while a full kitchen offers a menu that balances healthy choices with tasty comfort food alternatives. With an airy feel and lots of natural light, it's a great place to study or chat with friends. But what really catches your eye is that tiny box written in the bottom right-hand corner of the giant menu on the wall behind the counter: "Screw it – It's Cheat Day," the sign reads. Yes, here's a place that can be home-away-from-home.

Homegrown from the neighborhood, Egyptian-American Elenani describes himself as a "Brooklyn-born health freak and entrepreneur." Still a college student when he launched his first venture in 2013, his success was far from assured. "People thought I was crazy for setting up my business in this neighborhood," he remembers. "'All the ethnic groups only support their own community,' they'd say. I didn't listen."

Part of Elenani's success is due to his slow but steady approach. Starting with juice, then adding coffee, and finally the full kitchen, he was able to thrive while also defying the odds. "I didn't take any loans or investments. Instead, each business financed the next. Within four years, I had three successful Cocoa Grinder businesses, all in the same neighborhood." With franchises opening soon, the diverse crowd includes mothers with toddlers, seniors, students, and professionals.

The all-day breakfast offers eggs, french toast, pancakes, and granola. Salads, wraps, and bowls, plus an array of burgers make this a place to stop, relax, and "escape the grind."

Address 8511 3rd Avenue, Brooklyn, NY 11209, www.cocoagrindernyc.com (with several other locations) | Getting there Subway to 86 Street (R), walk one block west on 86th Street, then turn right onto 3rd Avenue | Hours Daily 7am–9pm | Tip Energized and ready to create? Pay a visit to the nearby Bay Ridge Art Space (86th Street between 3rd and 4th Avenues, Brooklyn, NY 11209, www.bayridgeartspace.com) for a private lesson from one of the two professional artists at this private studio. Children are welcome, too.

34 Coffee History in DUMBO

It's no wonder we all walk so fast

If Brooklyn has frequently moved to a different beat, part of the reason could be our long association with coffee. One man in particular, John Arbuckle, revolutionized the industry and, in the process, left a large footprint in DUMBO that can still be observed today.

Coming into its own as a popular beverage by the time of the Civil War, coffee's fortunes changed dramatically in 1864, when Jabez Burns invented a coffee roaster that sped up the average roasting time from a sack per half-hour to four sacks per 15 minutes, allowing producers to meet rising demand and make coffee an everyday drink instead of just one for special occasions.

Arbuckle, then in Pittsburgh, bought such a roaster and became the first to sell pre-roasted coffee by the pound, moving his production to DUMBO in 1886. "Coffee warehouses dotted the waterfront," explains Julie Golia, a public historian at the Brooklyn Historical Society (BHS) (see ch. 22). BHS's new annex is situated in Empire Stores, a remaining example of those 19th-century storehouses. "Importers would bring coffee to the waterfront, where the green coffee beans were taken into covered piers, then to the warehouse where they were inspected." Jim Munson, head of Brooklyn Roasting Company, believes Arbuckle is the most important figure in American coffee history: "He introduced ways to promote brand loyalty. Almost 80,000 people got their wedding rings from Arbuckle premiums. Plus, as a philanthropist, Arbuckle used his wealth to help others."

Golia notes that Arbuckle's real innovation, though, was in branding. "He created this idea of his coffee as the best, the purest, the most delicious coffee and sold it across the country." The remains of the company's private railroad, which transported the coffee to other cities, still exist in DUMBO's streets.

Address 53-83 Water Street, Brooklyn, NY 11201, www.empirestoresdumbo.com | Getting there Subway to High Street (A) or to York Street (F); ferry to DUMBO | Hours Daily 8am–7:30pm | Tip Visit the unique shops inside Empire Stores, starting with Natchie Art, a magical boutique filled with unique gift items made with the original drawings by artist and musician Nadia Ackerman (55 Water Street, Brooklyn, NY 11201, www.natchieart.com).

35 Cricket in Marine Park

The world's bat-and-ball game is welcome here

It can be difficult for Americans to understand the appeal of a game that can sometimes last for five days and end in a tie. Writer Bill Bryson once wrote in his travelogue about Australia, "In A Sunburned Country," that it is "the only sport in which a moderately active spectator burns as many calories as players – more if they are restless." Or, perhaps, there's a tendency to think cricketers look like dandies in their head-to-toe white uniforms, playing what they will sometimes refer to as "a gentleman's game" that involves "bowlers" (not pitchers) trying to achieve a "maiden" by hurling balls at batters holding a flattened bat wider than the one used in baseball, desperate not to be "dismissed."

But even if you don't know what a "googly" is, or you think a "golden duck" is a character in a fairy tale, you'll still enjoy heading out to this grassy expanse on a summer weekend afternoon to watch a match. Related to baseball in the way a distant cousin is family, cricket is a game of sounds and rhythms – the *thwack* of ball on bat, the *thrum* of fielders moving in pursuit of the hit ball, the staccato chatter of teammates as the play unfolds. Played on an oval field by teams of 11 players, each team bats in one long innings, with batsmen standing in front of a collection of wooden stumps (called a wicket) protecting it from being knocked down when the bowler flings the ball. Hitting the ball, which is in play in any direction, a batter may run toward a second wicket, trying to get there before the ball is caught or retrieved. Except for a wicket keeper (a catcher-like position), no one wears gloves. A game of modest pace, cricket is punctuated by bursts of dramatic intensity.

These weekend matches serve as a unique way for certain immigrant communities to retain a taste of life from home. Don't be afraid to ask questions; there will always be someone willing to explain finer points to the uninitiated.

Address Filmore Avenue and Marine Parkway, www.brooklyncricketleague.us | **Getting there** Subway to Neck Road (Q), walk to Avenue U–East 16th Street, then take the B 31 eastbound to Marine Park | **Hours** See website for match schedule | **Tip** The New York Parks Department also maintains cricket fields at Canarsie Park (Seaview Avenue and East 92nd Street) and Spring Creek Park (Gateway Drive off Erskine Street) (www.nycgovparks.org/facilities/cricket).

36 __ Crown Finish Caves

Giving "underground Brooklyn" new meaning

Not even many longtime Brooklynites are aware that a set of tunnels and caves exist under the heart of Crown Heights. Originally created in the 1860s as part of the operations for the old Nassau Brewery, the tunnels were used for lagering until 1914. After changing hands a few times, being used as a metal fabrication business and a moving and storage operation (neither of which used the tunnels), the building above the tunnels was purchased by Susan Boyle and Benton Brown in 2001. Still, the underground part of their property remained dormant for the first decade. They did visit the dark, subterranean spaces via a giant extension ladder, taking friends on tours, as ideas for how to utilize their caves fermented.

The turning point came when Benton took a course in Vermont on cheese production. "We came to understand the necessity for ripening the cheeses and got interested in the processes of aging," Susan recalled. "The caves are about 30 feet below street level, maintaining a constant temperature of 50°F and a super high humidity of around 95%. They are great for lagering beer and fermenting cheeses."

No cheeses are made on site. Instead, Crown Finish purchases "green" cheeses (typically one week old, before they have formed a rind) from regional producers, almost all within a five-hour drive of Brooklyn (think Vermont, Maine, Pennsylvania, and Upstate New York). In all, more than 25,000 pounds of cheese are on-site at any given time. A full list of the producers is available on their website.

Though most of their cheeses are produced for restaurants and the specialty cheese shop market, every other month, a sandwich board sign is placed outside, doors are thrown open, and locals have the chance to sample and buy these delectable treats in their Bergen Street lobby. Follow Crown Finish Caves closely on Instagram and Facebook for notice of these pop-up events.

Address 925 Bergen Street, Brooklyn, NY 11238, +1 (718)857-2717, www.crownfinishcaves.com, desk@crownfinishcaves.com | Getting there Subway to Nostrand Avenue (A), to Franklin Avenue, or Park Place (S) | Hours Events are posted on social media | Tip Some of Crown Finish Caves' cheeses are among the fine array of offerings at Stinky Bklyn (215 Smith Street, Brooklyn, NY 11231, www.stinkybklyn.com). The shop also features charcuterie and craft beer.

37__Dead Horse Bay

Where the past is only a tide away

Dead Horse Bay's name doesn't leave much to the imagination. The site of a series of slaughterhouses and horse-rendering factories that operated from the 1850s to the 1930s producing fertilizer and glue, at one time the inlet water was polluted with the rancid residues of ground animal bones and rotten flesh. Later, factories used fish oils produced from the menhaden, native to the bay, to tan leather. Associated smokestacks produced such potent fumes that an 1879 court order ruled that a local rail company could forbid anyone smelling of the smoke from riding their trains.

The bay was originally a salt marsh that was home to oyster beds harvested by Native Americans. By the 17th century, Dutch settlers established mills operated by the tidal waters. (A grindstone from one of these mills can be viewed along the Millstone Trail.) When the advent of the automotive age brought the death of the rendering industry, the bay became home to garbage incinerators and a landfill. During the 1920s, the entire surrounding area was raised 16 feet in order to create nearby Floyd Bennett Field. Slowly, these landfills have eroded, resulting in debris of all kinds washing upon the shores. Seashells and Victorian glass may wash up side by side, along with the occasional horse bone.

Bring water and wear sturdy shoes and comfortable clothes. From Flatbush Avenue, enter at an opening opposite the bus shelter at Floyd Bennett Drive. A Ranger Station is just up the road. The Millstone Trail lies left at the trail fork, while the rightmost trail leads to Glass Bottle Beach. The center Express Return Trail takes slightly longer (10–15 minutes total). Each trail ends in a sandy beach blanketed with the remnants of lives past.

Now part of the Gateway National Recreation Area, bird and animal species can be observed thriving in this now much cleaner national park.

Address Gateway National Park, Brooklyn, NY 11234, +1 (718)354-4606, www.nps.gov/gate/index.htm | Getting there Subway to Flatbush–Brooklyn College (2, or 5 at rush hour), then take bus Q35 to Floyd Bennett Field | Hours Sunrise to sunset | Tip Fishing is allowed by permit only at any of the beach areas accessed by these trails. Permits cost $50 per year and can be obtained at the Ryan Visitor Center (1 Floyd Bennett Field, Brooklyn, NY 11234, www.nps.gov/gate/planyourvisit/ryan-reopen.htm).

38 _Do The Right Thing_ Way
Walk on the set of a film masterpiece

With action that takes place over barely more than the course of one blisteringly hot summer day, Spike Lee's 1989 film *Do The Right Thing* distills and lays bare the racial tensions that seethe just below the surface on a single block of Bedford-Stuyvesant. Sal, a middle-aged Italian-American, has owned a small pizzeria for 25 years. His two grown sons, Pino and Vito, now help run the business. Pino makes clear that he doesn't like that the shop is in an African-American neighborhood and is open about his racist feelings toward the people who live on the street. He especially dislikes Mookie, a twentysomething young father who works as the pizzeria's delivery man and who, unlike Sal and his sons, lives in the community. As the day heats up, tempers increasingly fray until, near nightfall, Mookie takes things into his own hands. The result: one of the most compelling endings in cinematic history, earning it a place on the National Film Registry.

DTRT's cast included Danny Aiello, John Turturro, Giancarlo Esposito, Rosie Perez, and the legendary Ozzie Davis and Ruby Dee, acting alongside Lee himself as Mookie. It's no wonder that critics Siskel and Ebert both agreed and gave the movie two enthusiastic thumbs up, naming it a Top 10 film for the year. DTRT Way was proclaimed in July 2015.

While you won't find Sal's famous pizzeria (it was constructed on an empty lot at Stuyvesant and Lexington, then torn down after shooting), a quick walk along the block lets you see several other important locations that remain. Mookie's home is at 173 Stuyvesant, near Quincy Street. Directly across the street, at 184, an added façade transformed the brownstone into Yes Jesus Last Baptist Church. 174 played home to FM108 We Love Radio, with the DJ played by Samuel L. Jackson. Finally, the window at 167 found Ruby Dee's Mother Sister surveying life on the street.

Address Stuyvesant Avenue between Quincy Avenue and Lexington Avenue, Brooklyn, NY 11221 | Getting there Subway to Myrtle Avenue (J, M), to Kosciuszko Street (J) | Hours Unrestricted from the outside only | Tip Spike Lee's production company, Forty Acres and A Mule, maintains production offices in Fort Greene (75 South Elliott Place, Brooklyn, NY 11217, www.40acres.com). For the past two years, Lee has spearheaded the "Prince Born Day Purple People Party," a Brooklyn dance party to celebrate the late artist Prince near his birthday on June 7th.

39__Drummer's Grove

Be prepared to move at this weekend tradition

Don't worry if you forget your map on the way to find this long-standing tribute to percussion in Prospect Park: just follow the pulsing rhythms to the home of this regular weekend event that has become such an institution that the Park Alliance has provided permanent seating for participants and observers. Begun in 1968 and situated along the southeast edge of the park near the LeFrak Center at Lakeside, several generations of bangers and thumpers have deployed drums, bongos, djembes, bodhráns, talking drums, and even plastic buckets to keep the beat.

On any given day, you can see – and hear – drummers from nearly every segment of Brooklyn's broad world map of residents, inhabiting this space. Though hailing from far-flung regions of the globe or corners of the borough, here they become one as the "Congo Square drummers." The name comes from the place in New Orleans where African slaves would go to drum on Sundays, keeping their traditions alive. It's not uncommon to witness a share of the gathered audience dancing to the hypnotic, polyrhythmic cadence, especially kids. More experienced percussionists lend support to novices. Everyone is welcome to join in. More than almost anything else, Drummer's Grove demonstrates that Prospect is truly the people's park.

After, be sure to stroll up to the LeFrak Center at Lakeside. Grab a bite and a drink at the Bluestone Café, then lace on some skates – roller skates in summer months and ice skates in winter. Indoor and outdoor seating offers picturesque views of the lake. Bikes and boats are also available for rent. (Season passes are available for all of these activities. Check the website for details.) The Splash Pad, a playground featuring 20 waterjets' worth of fun (at no charge, water shoes are recommended) for kids under 12 and their caregivers, operates May–September – it's the perfect way to beat the heat.

Address Prospect Park, near Parkside Avenue and Ocean Avenue, Brooklyn, NY 11225, +1 (718)965-8951, www.nycgo.com/venues/prospect-park-drummers-grove | Getting there Subway to Parkside Avenue (Q) | Hours Apr–Oct 2–7pm | Tip Keur Djembe African Drum Shop in Park Slope has been selling West African drums since 1998. The shop also offers drumming workshops and drum repair services (568 Union Street, Brooklyn, NY 11215, www.keurdjembe.com).

40__Ebbets Field Site

Brooklyn's Field of Dreams

"There used to be a ballpark," Frank Sinatra sang, evoking nostalgia for a long-gone, simpler time. For many, that ballpark was Ebbets Field, home to the Brooklyn Dodgers. Dubbed "Dem Bums" by sports cartoonist Willard Mullin after he overheard a taxi driver ask "How did dem bums do today?" the team's record of futility made, "Wait til next year," a fan lament.

Charles Ebbets, who began his association with the team selling tickets, programs and peanuts in 1883 when the team played in Washington Park (see ch. 20), eventually bought the Dodgers and hoped to build a big, new stadium near Brooklyn's trolley lines. For several years, Ebbets secretly acquired lots in Pigtown, a local dump. By 1911, he had enough land. Selling half his Dodger shares to finance the stadium, he soon built Brooklyn a new 25,000-seat stadium at Sullivan Place, near the corner of Empire Boulevard and Bedford Avenue. The Dodgers won the first game, an exhibition played April 5, 1913 against crosstown rival Yankees, 3-2 in front of more than 30,000 fans. At a repeat faceoff two days later, on a cold spring day, Brooklyn's nine lost in front of only 1,000.

The Dodgers' perennial struggles all changed in the postwar era, with a line-up that included Hall of Fame legends like Jackie Robinson, Pee Wee Reese, Gil Hodges, Don Newcombe, Duke Snyder, and Roy Campanella. Between 1947, when Robinson arrived and broke the color barrier, and 1956, the team won six National League pennants and one World Series. That championship, in 1955 against the mighty Yankees, rewarded the loyal, long-suffering Dodger fanbase.

The team moved to Los Angeles after the 1957 season, and the hole in Brooklyn's heart never healed. On February 23, 1960, the stadium was demolished. All that remains now is an small marker erected in 1962 near the entrance to the apartments built over the Ebbets Field site.

Address Find marker at 1700 Bedford Avenue, Brooklyn, NY 11225. The stadium lay in the area bounded by Montgomery Street, McKeever Place, and Sullivan Place. | **Getting there** Subway to Prospect Park (B, Q) | **Hours** Unrestricted | **Tip** During those early years of the ballpark, Charles Ebbets lived a short walk away from the stadium (193 Ocean Avenue, Brooklyn, NY 11225). He was buried in Green-Wood Cemetery upon his death in 1925. The cemetery periodically offers baseball-themed tours, including Ebbets' grave (www.green-wood.com).

41 — Elephant Electrocution

The story that sparked the animal rights movement

Coney Island is a land of sideshows, curios, and oddities. But, even so, the story of Topsy the Elephant qualifies as strange-but-true. A female Asian elephant illegally smuggled into the country by the Forepaugh Circus, a competitor to Ringling Brothers and Barnum & Bailey, Topsy was (falsely) advertised as the "first baby elephant born on American soil" and toured with the circus for over 25 years.

By 1902, a fully grown Topsy was neither small nor cuddly at 10 feet tall, 20 feet long, and about 5 tons in weight. Unfortunately, she also had acquired a reputation for being bad, not all of which was deserved. Performing in Brooklyn that May, Topsy threw a spectator who wandered into the holding tent to the ground and then stomped him to death. The killing made for great tabloid headlines and contributed to Topsy's sale a month later to a Coney Island impresario. In fact, the dead man was drunk and had thrown sand in Topsy's face and burned her trunk with a lit cigar.

More misadventure followed. Topsy's drunken trainer stabbed her with a pitchfork, unharnessed her, and allowed her to roam alone through the streets and alleys of Coney Island. Now labeled unmanageable, Topsy's owners decided to put her to death. But, in one last effort to squeeze money out of her, they announced that the poor pachyderm would be hanged in Luna Park, with spectators charged 25¢ a head. Protests by the burgeoning ASPCA resulted in some changes. Topsy would be executed in an invitation-only event that combined poisoning, hanging, and electrocution to bring about her demise.

So it was that on January 4, 1903, fifteen hundred spectators gathered to witness Topsy's gruesome death. The end came swiftly. While there is no marker commemorating the event today, Topsy's life and death brought animal welfare and the concept of animal rights to the fore in the United States.

Address 1000 Surf Avenue, Brooklyn, NY 11224 | Getting there Subway to Coney Island–Stillwell Avenue (D, F, N, Q) | Hours Variable, see website for daily hours | Tip Topsy's death was recorded by Thomas Edison's film company. The 74-second *Electrocuting an Elephant* was widely available for viewing on kinescopes. It can be viewed today at the Coney Island USA Museum (1208 Surf Avenue, Brooklyn, NY 11224, www.coneyisland.com/programs/coney-island-museum).

42 Emily Roebling Plaques
The woman behind Brooklyn's Great Bridge

Largely overlooked by history for her critical role in the construction of Brooklyn's Great Bridge, Emily Roebling didn't merit an obituary in *The New York Times* when she died in 1903, a fact not corrected until the paper published one belatedly... in 2018! Yet, without her, it's nearly impossible to imagine the project's completion. Part secretary, procurement officer, site manager, and political dealmaker from the mid-1870s until the bridge opened in 1883, Emily Roebling had a hand in every aspect of the historic venture.

"Colonel Roebling, as he was known, was no desk engineer," Erica Wagner, author of *Chief Engineer: Washington Roebling, The Man Who Built The Brooklyn Bridge* (2017), notes. "In the early 1870s the work began to affect him very badly. When the Brooklyn caisson was being constructed he was in the chamber as much as any man who worked for him. He was afflicted by 'caisson disease' – decompression sickness, or 'the bends' – causing terrible pain." According to Wagner, Emily was the only person the now-bedridden colonel could tolerate. "She became, if you like, a bridge between her husband and the world: his assistant engineers, the trustees of the bridge, the men in control of the money."

Wagner balks at the notion of Emily as an engineer but feels that it "does not diminish her role. That forces her into a masculine paradigm of achievement; as if her role as Washington's wife is to be discounted – as women's work so often is, even today." For her efforts, Emily Roebling was afforded the honor of being the first person to cross the bridge, riding an open carriage and holding a live rooster as a sign of victory.

When you walk over the bridge, look for the plaques on each tower erected in 1951 by the Brooklyn Engineers Club, that commemorate her achievement: "Back of every great work we can find the self-sacrificing devotion of a woman."

THE BUILDERS OF THE BRIDGE
DEDICATED TO THE MEMORY OF
EMILY WARREN ROEBLING
1843 - 1903
WHOSE FAITH AND COURAGE HELPED HER STRICKEN HUSBAND
COL WASHINGTON A. ROEBLING, C.E.
1837 - 1926
COMPLETE THE CONSTRUCTION OF THIS BRIDGE
FROM THE PLANS OF HIS FATHER
JOHN A. ROEBLING, C.E.
1806 - 1869
WHO GAVE HIS LIFE TO THE BRIDGE

"BACK OF EVERY GREAT WORK WE CAN FIND
THE SELF-SACRIFICING DEVOTION OF A WOMAN"

THIS TABLET ERECTED 1951 BY
THE BROOKLYN ENGINEERS CLUB
WITH FUNDS RAISED BY POPULAR SUBSCRIPTION

Address The towers of the Brooklyn Bridge, via the pedestrian entrance at the intersection of Adams Street and Tillary Street, Brooklyn, NY 11201 | Getting there Subway to Jay Street–MetroTech (A, C, F, R), to Borough Hall (2, 3, 4, 5), or to Court Street (N, R) | Hours Unrestricted | Tip In Anchorage Plaza (the intersection of Hicks Street and Old Fulton Street, Brooklyn, NY 11201) is the work, *Roebling Family Sculpture*, honoring John, Washington, and Emily Roebling, by Keith Godard, a British artist working in DUMBO.

43 Emmons Avenue Charters

Deep-sea fishing Brooklyn style

To paraphrase philosopher and ecologist Henry David Thoreau, people go fishing all their lives without knowing that fish aren't really what they're after. Whether that happens to be true or not, several boats operating from launches along this stretch of Emmons Avenue offer opportunities to test your mettle on the open water, and time to contemplate what it is you hope to catch.

Ocean Eagle V's family-owned operation offers a comfortable 8-hour day out on the sea in an 80-foot vessel. With more than a quarter century of experience on fishing, commercial, and party boats, captain Greg Nardiello will make you feel at home, whether you're a novice or experienced fisherperson. Knowledgeable about where the best spots are, he tries hard to make certain that customers leave the day with success. He also narrates some of the action, providing insight into how a seasoned veteran of these voyages reads the sea. The website contains fishing reports that will keep you aware of whether it's porgy, sea bass, or trigger fish that are likely to be the catch of the day. Captain Greg's experienced crew are on-hand to offer advice, humor and moral support.

Another boat, the *Marilyn Jean IV* at Pier 6, makes two 8-hour trips daily: most mornings from 7am–3pm and night fishing from 7pm–midnight. It's a 70-foot party boat, and, as with the *Ocean Eagle V*, you'll only need to bring yourself, as rods, reels, hooks and sinkers, and bait are all provided. Heating allows the vessel to take excursions out late into the season.

Most visitors don't know that Sheepshead Bay is named for an edible fish that was once abundant in the bay waters but is now increasingly rare. This area was severely hit by Hurricane Sandy in late October 2012, and the tidal surge extended as far inland as Avenue X and reached as high as 10 feet above ground. Flood waters caused millions of dollars in damage and took months to repair.

Address Ocean Eagle V, 2250 Emmons Avenue, Brooklyn, NY 11235, +1 (917)669-2985, www.oceaneaglev.com; Marilyn Jean IV, 2200 Emmons Avenue, Brooklyn, NY 11235, +1 (917)650-3212, www.mj2fishing.com | Getting there Subway to Sheepshead Bay (Q) | Hours See website for schedules | Tip The New York City Ferry service, run by the MTA, offers spectacularly scenic routes and beach excursions for the same price as a subway ride (www.ferry.nyc).

44 ESPO's Art World

Art as the voice of a community

It's difficult to pin down exactly what ESPO's Art World is. Created in 2012, it's part workshop and gallery, part studio and print shop, and part community center. Studio manager Matthew Kuborn calls it, "a base of operations." In other words, it's all of those things at once. Really, ESPO's is less about what it *is* than what it *does*.

ESPO is the artistic persona of Stephen Powers (ES plus PO, based on his initials). A native of Philadelphia, Powers began as a graffiti writer in his teens back in the late 1980s. But Kenny Meez, "style counsel," who has worked with Powers for about 30 years, says the artist was always thinking about the next step. "While everyone else was using cans of spray paint, he started to use house paints and rollers," he says. "He started a magazine. When I asked Steve why, he said 'Because we've got something to say.'"

Words are often featured on his canvases. Using irony, sarcasm, and plain speech, Powers' artistic brush mixes traditional sign painting, print advertising, and pop art in a unique blend he calls "visual blues." It's an apt description. Like the blues, Powers is echoing the voice of the community around him, and in conversation with the group of artists who form the ESPO's community. "Steve makes it a point to involve the people and the neighborhoods where he works. Rather than being an artist who puts himself and his work on a pedestal, there's a grassroots, street-level process to the art," Meez adds. ESPO's produces signs for local businesses and banners for a neighborhood outreach center, and holds regular printing workshops where anyone can bring a shirt and have it silk screened at no cost.

There's also work for sale, with an emphasis on making the art affordable – and relevant – for all. For Powers, art is about making personal things universal and making universal things personal, be that a lithograph, a tote bag, or a roll of toilet paper with a clever quip.

Address 72 4th Avenue, Brooklyn, NY 11217, +1 (929)295-0427, www.firstandfifteenth.net, espoprints@gmail.com | Getting there Subway to Atlantic Avenue–Barclays Center (B, N, Q, R, 2, 3, 4, or 5) | Hours Daily noon–6pm | Tip *All I Need is YOU … and New Shoes*, a mural by Powers, covers a wall near the intersection of Bond Street and Dekalb Avenue.

45 Essen New York Deli

Keeping a tasty cultural tradition alive

Michael Jacobowitz, owner of this traditional kosher deli in West Midwood, jokes that he's the last man standing. While that may not be literally true, it is fair to say that the old-school delicatessen experience is becoming increasingly a thing of the past. "We are one of the last *glatt kosher* delis, processing all of our meat in-house," he boasts, referring to a specific inspection process that allows the food to adhere to strict Jewish dietary laws. "We brine our own tongues and corned beef, and smoke our own pastrami, briskets, and roast beefs. Every single delicatessen item is made within the four walls of our store from scratch. Nobody does this today because – believe it or not – making your own is more expensive than buying it already produced."

Part of why Jacobowitz does it this way comes from personal pride. "If I wasn't doing it homemade, I would be embarrassed. I grew up going to delis as a kid, and if you call yourself a deli, you've got to do it right." Adding to this sense is Essen New York's "family lineage" to one of the city's legendary Jewish eateries, Schmulka Bernstein's. A fixture on Essex Street in the Lower East Side, when the deli closed up shop in the late 80s, an attempt was made to recreate it (tables, chairs, and all) in Brooklyn on Coney Island Avenue. Jacobowitz bought that iteration in 2010 and renamed it, playing on the Yiddish word *essen*, meaning "to eat."

Jacobowitz also notes that he never skimps on portions, which also wins new customers and keeps old timers coming back. So do the traditional recipes for items like Hungarian stuffed cabbage, *kreplach* and matzo ball soups ("Jewish penicillin," he jokes), and *kishke* (meat and meal encased in a beef intestine) served with gravy.

"When people see a family-run business, families like to come in," Jacobowitz adds. "It's a homey atmosphere, and that's what delis are all about."

Address 1359 Coney Island Avenue, Brooklyn, NY 11230, +1 (718)859-1002, www.essennydeli.com | Getting there Subway to Avenue J (Q) | Hours Sun–Wed 11am–11pm, Thu 11–1am, Fri 11am–2pm | Tip Looking for kosher ingredients to make your favorite dishes at home? Visit Pomegranate (507 Coney Island Avenue, Brooklyn, NY 11230) just up the street. The grocer employs three full-time on-site *mashgiachs* (supervisors of the laws of kosher) to monitor its kitchens.

46 The EX-LAX Building

Keeping things moving on Atlantic Avenue

You'll be forgiven if you do a double-take while passing by this building as you stroll through Boerum Hill. One of the first factory co-op conversions when transformed into a 58-unit building in 1981, these now luxury apartments, drooled over for their high ceilings and prime location, began life as corporate headquarters to the well-known laxative. Hungarian immigrant Max Kiss, who came penniless to the United States at 16 and later trained as a pharmacist at Columbia University, invented the product by combining a tasteless powder discovered by Bayer with chocolate. Kiss took the name from the phrase "Excellent Laxative," although it also bore a striking resemblance to "Ex Laz," a phrase used in connection with the stalemated Hungarian parliament. Old timers in the neighborhood recall the signs on the side of the building that read, "The Ideal Laxative."

The tasty and effective product was a hit, and by 1925 operations were so successful that this large factory was built to accommodate production. What's lesser known is that Ex-Lax also housed its research labs here, maintaining test monkeys in cages on the factory roof. Legend has it that the monkeys would periodically escape from their cages, wreaking havoc along the way. A *New York Times* piece on the building included a memory from a former employee who called them – with empathy – "the vilest-tempered monkeys you've ever seen." It's certainly easy to understand why.

While you're here, check out the graffiti mural that adorns the Flatbush Avenue sides of two buildings between State and Schermerhorn Streets. Painted by Brooklyn artist Katie Merz, the white-on-black mural transforms the wall into a playful chalkboard, covered in words, places, names, and icons related to Brooklyn. Stylistically, the work pays visual homage to 1980s' artistic icons Keith Haring and Jean-Michel Basquiat. Not to be missed!

Address 423 – 443 Atlantic Avenue, Brooklyn, NY 11217 | **Getting there** Subway to Atlantic Avenue–Barclays Center (2, 3, 4, 5, B, Q), to Pacific Street (D, N, R), or to Hoyt–Schermerhorn Streets (A, C, G) | **Hours** Unrestricted from the outside only | **Tip** If food is the best medicine, go to Brooklyn Farmacy and Soda Fountain (513 Henry Street, Brooklyn, NY 11231, www.brooklynfarmacyandsodafountain.com). Housed in a 1920s' apothecary store, this restaurant has everything your grandpa loved: from pastrami and grilled cheese to egg creams and whoopie pies – but with a modern twist.

47 __ Farrell's Bar and Grill

If you need a seat, you're too drunk to be served

The illuminated neon sign outside this Windsor Terrace fixture lets you know right away you're in for a bit of a trip in a time machine. The "grill" is long gone. Inside, a plaque tells you that Farrell's was established in 1933. The wooden ledges all around the place are from a time when there weren't any stools – and there still aren't many. The reason: if you needed a seat, you were clearly too drunk to be served. In the back, there are a handful of tables and a jukebox. The bar is framed with mini Stars and Stripes, and banners for the branches of the military and the Coast Guard. There are the neatly arranged rows of spirits bottles, though they are perhaps more workmanlike in selection and number, and five beer taps. Next to the cash register, there's a sign taped up on the bar mirror that says they don't accept credit cards. Just for emphasis, another sign has a picture of The Man in Black that reads "Cash Only."

Farrell's is the kind of Irish bar that people tell stories about. Legend has it that the bar was the first in the city to nab a liquor license after Prohibition ended. There's the one about how no women were served here until the 70s when writer Pete Hamill arrived with actress Shirley MacLaine. Audaciously, she just went to the bar, ordered a drink, and that was that. Writer Jimmy Breslin was another fabled regular, drinking with the legion of cops and firefighters who called the bar home. You can still order up "a container" – a 32-ounce cup (traditionally made of styrofoam). With a lid snapped on, they can be legally carried outside even filled with beer.

For another Irish bar in Brooklyn, try Chinatown's Soccer Tavern (6004 Eighth Avenue). Originally a speakeasy in 1929, it offers the kind of cultural mash-up that gives the borough its unique character and maintains a comfortable neighborhood ambiance. It also offers large TV screens for watching the big game and a dart board for one-on-one matches.

Address 215 Prospect Park West, Brooklyn, NY 11215, +1 (718)788-8779 | Getting there Subway to 15th Street–Prospect Park (F, G) | Hours Daily 10–4am | Tip Teddy's Bar and Grill (96 Berry Street, Brooklyn, NY 11249, www.teddys.nyc) is the venerable grandfather of Brooklyn bars. After more than 130 years, it is the oldest bar in continual operation. Lovingly restored to its period charm, it has been featured in shows including *Boardwalk Empire*, *The Good Wife*, and *King of New York*.

48 Flatbush Reformed Church

Brooklyn's holy ground for more than 350 years

Founded in 1654 on the directive of New Netherlands' last governor, Peter Stuyvesant, this church sitting in the heart of busy commercial Flatbush represents the waning days of Dutch New World colonialism. Originally ordered to be a wooden building constructed in the shape of the cross in the town of Midwout ("middle wood"), the current church is the third structure built on the site from of a combination of local metamorphic schist (the ancient bedrock) and brick. It rests upon the stone foundation created in 1699 for the second building.

Designed in the Federal style by Thomas Fardon and built in 1793–98, the stately edifice nevertheless remains one of the oldest in the borough. Reportedly, the sanctuary sits atop the remains of American Revolutionary War soldiers slain in the Battle of Brooklyn. Inside, a set of stained-glass windows created by Tiffany Studios and installed in 1889 commemorate the early Dutch settlers who founded the church.

Topped by a steeple containing a bell imported from Holland, the church was the center of early community life. A courthouse stood nearby, as did a school across the street, later replaced by Erasmus Hall Academy in 1786. Stroll in the graveyard behind the church, where some of the borough's oldest family names are inscribed upon the tombstones, including Lefferts, Ditmas, Van Sicklen, and Vanderveer.

The church was one of three founded by Stuyvesant a mere decade before the Dutch surrender of New Netherlands to the British. All still remain. Flatlands Dutch Reformed Church (3931 Flatbush Avenue) occupies a Greek Revivalist building constructed in 1848, containing another historic cemetery and a church bell that rings to mark the death of every US president. Meanwhile, Old First Reformed Church is now located at 729 Carroll Street in Park Slope.

Address 890 Flatbush Avenue, Brooklyn, NY 11226, +1 (718)284-5140 | **Getting there** Subway to Church Avenue (Q) | **Hours** Weekly services Sun 11am | **Tip** Visit the Wyckoff House Museum (5816 Clarendon Avenue, Brooklyn, NY 11203, www.wyckoffmuseum.org) for another site related to Dutch colonial Brooklyn. The 1652 one-room farmhouse, home to Pieter and Grietje Claesen, still stands as part of the expanded and reconfigured structure that, restored, is open to visit in East Flatbush. Claesen is buried beneath the pulpit of the Flatlands Church.

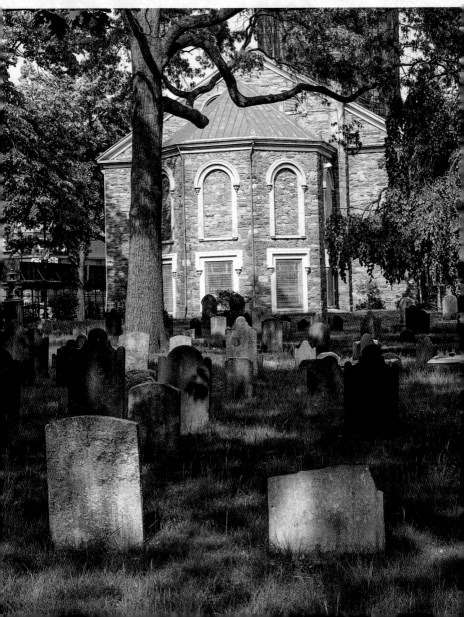

49__ The Floasis
The point is not to feel the burn

"At the end of our 8-week cycle of classes, we have a 'fire graduation,' where participants get to burn. It's pretty exciting." Lydia Darling, director of operations of this Bushwick-based community, is describing a commencement ceremony like few others. It marks the completion of a journey newcomers to The Floasis undertake as students at the only school of fire arts sanctioned by the Fire Department of New York. Individual sessions (typically capped at six students) focus on different techniques, using instruments like hula hoops, double staffs, or poi (tethered weights swung in rhythmic fashion). A session on fire safety ensures that students get comfortable with performing the movements to minimize risk.

When all the prep work is completed, Darling says, props are soaked in fuel appropriate for the circumstances, and then students get to burn. "At The Floasis, we always have people with safety equipment standing by," she notes. "For some people, burning is meditative. For others, it is performance, so there is almost a dance, a choreography. We have a community that runs the entire range, from novice, to hobbyist, to professional. Everyone is welcome."

Founded by Tara McManus in 2011, who also designs and produces a line of fire-retardant clothing, the group aims to maintain a venue that supports what have become known as the Flow Arts. Given that fire can trigger fear and discomfort, achieving equilibrium can be a challenge, let alone control and mastery. So the somewhat poetic term "flow" embodies both the sense of ultimate awareness that comes from being completely in the moment and the movement through that moment, or the sense of "going with the flow."

The Floasis hosts regular events to demonstrate the fire arts. The recent Combustion NYC! took place in Maria Hernandez Park and was the first openly accessible fire show ever permitted by FDNY.

Address 1342A Dekalb Avenue, Brooklyn, NY 11221, www.thefloasis.com, floasisHQ@gmail.com | Getting there Subway to Central Avenue (M) | Hours Check the website for class and event schedules | Tip For entertaining performances, some of which incorporate fire-eating or fire-breathing, come one, come all to Coney Island USA's Circus Sideshow (1208 Surf Avenue, Brooklyn, NY 11224, www.coneyisland.com).

50 Flocks of Monk Parrots

Brooklyn's South American connection

If you find yourself wondering about the noisy squawking and chattering going on overhead, you may just have encountered members of one of Brooklyn's more unusual immigrant communities. Urban legend says wild monk parakeets, small green subtropical birds also known as Quaker parrots, first appeared in Brooklyn when a crate being used to transport them from their native Argentina opened while at JFK Airport. More likely, says Stephen Baldwin, author of *Brooklyn Parrots FAQ*, birds escaped, or were released by owners and pet shops, a few at a time over several years. "In the 1960s and 1970s, exotic parrots of all kinds were being sent into the US by the thousands each year. Monk Parakeets were part of this forced great migration." Baldwin estimates that more than 65,000 monks arrived in the United States during this period, most of them from Argentina, where they were regarded as pests.

Resourceful team players, monk parakeets build their own nests, usually from sticks, on telephone poles and electric transformers or among branches rather than relying on holes in trees. They're non-migratory, so these nests serve as home throughout the year. "Brooklyn is about the same distance north of the equator as Argentina is to the south, so they don't mind New York winters so much," Baldwin notes.

Though small groupings of monk parakeets have been observed throughout the borough, the colonies at Green-Wood Cemetery and Brooklyn College are currently the most constant. Baldwin estimates about 30 to 40 birds reside at each, though numbers fluctuate. "Monk parakeet flocks have been known to split when the population grows so large that either nest space or food sources begin to be stressed." At Green-Wood, look for the parrots among the spires of the ornate Gothic entry gate. The Brooklyn College colony has built nests among the light towers around the soccer field.

Address Various, www.brooklynparrots.com, stephencarlbaldwin@gmail.com |
Getting there Subway to 25 Street (R) for Green-Wood Cemetery, or to Flatbush
Avenue–Brooklyn College (2, 5) | Hours Unrestricted | Tip Stephen Baldwin offers
monthly parrot "safaris" to observe the birds in the Brooklyn wilds. For details, visit
his website (www.brooklynparrots.com).

51 French Connection Chase
Do not try this at home

Jimmy "Popeye" Doyle, an undercover narcotics cop, shot at and now in hot pursuit, flags down a car on a gritty 1970s' street in Bensonhurst. Flashing his badge and commandeering the vehicle for police business, Doyle hops in the dirty brown Pontiac and swiftly gives chase. Above, the elevated subway cars rumble onward with the gun-wielding hitman aboard the Manhattan-bound train, desperate to escape. Ahead of Doyle lies an obstacle course of cars, pedestrians, and girders to dodge, race through, and thread.

So begins one of cinema's most famous – and harrowing – car chase scenes, the centerpiece of the 1971 police thriller, *The French Connection*. Directed by William Friedkin (winner of the Oscar for Best Director for this effort), the film was based on a 1969 nonfiction account of two NYPD officers' efforts to unmask those behind an international drug trafficking operation. Starring Gene Hackman, who won Best Actor as the intrepid Popeye Doyle, Roy Scheider as his partner Buddy "Cloudy" Russo, and Fernando Rey as heroin smuggler Alain Charnier, the film became the first R-rated movie to win an Academy Award for Best Picture.

Not in the original script, the car chase was the brainchild of producer Philip D'Antonio, who wanted to top the gripping sequence of his earlier film, *Bullitt*. The problem: the film crew did not have the proper permit from the city to proceed. Audacious improv followed. Stunt driver Bill Hickman strapped in with Friedkin in the backseat holding the camera, and they set out under the tracks running from Bay 50th Street to 62nd Street Station along Stillwell Avenue, at speeds sometimes approaching 90 miles per hour! Despite some close calls, including sideswiping a city bus and an accident with a local driver, the resulting scene is six minutes of cinematic gold, ending with Doyle shooting the fleeing hitman as he ascends the subway steps.

Address Several locations beginning at the Marlboro Housing Project at Stillwell Avenue and Avenue W and ending at 62nd Street Station at the intersection of New Utrecht Avenue and 14th Avenue | Getting there Stillwell Avenue under the D train elevated rail, along 86th Street and New Utrecht Avenue, to the 62nd Street station, Brooklyn | Hours Unrestricted | Tip John Dewey High School, located just behind the Bay 50th Street Station, counts filmmaker Spike Lee (see ch. 38) among its alumni (50 Avenue X, Brooklyn, NY 11223, www.johndeweyhighschool.org).

52 __ Gaga at Mark Morris

Your hips are your motor now

A form of modern-contemporary dance from Israel that doesn't require any prior technical knowledge of dance, Gaga is a fun and creative way to explore space and connect with your body when hectic city life feels like it's closing in all around you. Combining elements of dance with yoga, Gaga classes at the Mark Morris Dance Group studios in the heart of Fort Greene's cultural district will leave you energized, refreshed, and reinvigorated.

Developed by Ohad Naharin, formerly the artistic director of the Batsheva Dance Company founded by Martha Graham in the early 1960s, the practice of Gaga centers heavily on mental and emotional presence, but ultimately the key is movement. Sign up for a class online under Modern-Contemporary Dance. You can also join a class as a walk-in at the desk. Many are open for beginners. Gaga/people sessions are for dancers and non-dancers alike. Be sure to wear comfortable clothes and expect to dance barefoot.

The class is a feast of expressive motion, with everyone constantly exploring the dance space, listening to their natural rhythms, and encountering organically what it is that our individual bodies do. It will come as a relief to find there aren't routines to learn or instructors barking "Kick!" "Step!" or "Spin!" A lack of mirrors creates a space where there is less temptation to compare yourself with others and less tendency to imagine any one way of moving as "right." Instead, class teachers lead gently, using visual imagery or calling your attention to spaces in the room, suggesting parts of your body that are "your motor" to guide you.

This relatively freeform approach opens a space for unconventional ideas of what it means to dance that even the most self-conscious wallflowers will appreciate. The result is a compelling, hour-long, personal, and communal experience that will never be replicated in another Gaga class.

Address 3 Lafayette Avenue, Brooklyn, NY 11217, +1 (718)624-8400, www.markmorrisdancegroup.org, info@mmdg.org | **Getting there** Subway to Nevins Street (2, 3, 4, 5), to Lafayette Avenue (C), to Fulton Street (G), or to Atlantic Avenue–Barclays Center (2, 3, 4, 5, B, D, N, Q, R, W) | **Hours** See website for class schedules | **Tip** Close by, the Barclays Center boasts a green roof, 135,000 square feet covered in sedum to absorb rain water and support the storm water system and to contribute accoustically to the venue (620 Atlantic Avenue, Brooklyn, NY 11217, www.barclayscenter.com).

53__Gleason's Gym

The cathedral of boxing is open for all to attend

Jake LaMotta. Roberto Duran. Larry Holmes. Mike Tyson. Muhammad Ali. These are just some of the iconic world champions who honed their skills training at this legendary gym during its fabled 80-year history. Founded by an Italian-American bantamweight who changed his name from Gagliardi to Gleason in order to attract support within New York's Irish community, the gym (now located in the heart of fashionable DUMBO) still prepares boxers to the highest standards. According to current owner Bruce Silverblade, seven world champions currently train here on a regular basis. But, what might surprise you, he says, is the sense of community that many people find while they're punching bags or sparring in a ring.

"The fighters come into the gym to get out of their daily environments. They come here to box," the owner observes. "Meanwhile, I have wealthy Wall Street execs coming in. Both meet people that they don't normally associate with and get to know them as human beings." Beginner or world champion, members enjoy the sense of belonging here. "Everyone pays the same. If Mike Tyson were in here training and he wanted a heavy bag that you were on, he'd have to wait for you."

When Silverblade became part owner in 1984, the gym was exclusively filled with pro and amateur fighters. These days, gym membership is about 85% people boxing for fitness training. Women currently make up about a quarter of that number. "The women are tremendous competitors," he says. "They train hard – harder than the men. They say, 'Teach me how to box.' So you start from zero and you train them, while guys who come in here want to appear macho and tough. It may take a couple of months for them to be ready to start actually learning how to box."

Silverblade encourages people to drop in. Don't be surprised if you end up looking at photos and hearing stories about the greats.

Address 130 Water Street, Brooklyn, NY 11201, +1 (718)797-2872, www.gleasonsgym.com |
Getting there Subway to York Street (F), or to High Street–Brooklyn Bridge (A) | Hours
Mon–Fri 5am–10pm, Sat & Sun 8am–6pm | Tip Undisputed heavyweight champ Mike
Tyson grew up in Bed-Stuy and Brownsville, living as a young boy in an apartment building,
where he kept pigeons on the building's rooftop (178 Amboy Street, Brooklyn, NY 11212).

54_ Gotham Archery

Slings and arrows, not at an outrageous fortune

While on the outside this place may look like just another Gowanus warehouse, open the door and you might just have found the place to channel your inner Katniss Everdeen or Robin Hood. With a range that can accommodate 40 shooters aiming at targets from 5 to 20 yards in distance, Gotham Archery offers the chance to trade the daily frenzy for quiet concentration. "Each shot is an opportunity to pull back and let it all go," general manager Megan Del Prior says, explaining the appeal of what many would see as a rural sport for urban dwellers. "All that stress, all the bad stuff... Letting it go is what archery is all about."

An hour-long introductory lesson, easy to book through the website, is the place to begin, and it starts with 15 minutes of safety tips. As you can imagine, stance, posture, and etiquette are all essential to master from the beginning to maintain a secure environment. All of the equipment is available to borrow, so there's no need for a hefty investment beforehand.

Bows primarily come in two types. Recurves are the long and slender "S" shaped bows, usually made of fiberglass or wood and used for Olympic archery. Compound bows tend to be a bit heavier and use a system of pulleys and cables to produce powerful, consistent shots. While you'll be able to try them both, Megan says it's not uncommon to have a preference. "It's like something out of *Harry Potter* – usually the bow calls you. You'll know which one's for you by the end of the day."

The club holds regular tournaments in which people of all sizes, shapes, and abilities can compete. Archery provides the rare chance for women and men to compete against each other, and people of different ages, too. Bored with paper targets? There's 3D shooting on Mondays, where it's anything from toy turkeys to velociraptors! Or, steel yourself and take a knife- or ax-throwing lesson or two.

Address 480 Baltic Street, Brooklyn, NY 11217, +1 (718)858-5060, www.got-archery.com, info@got-archery.com | Getting there Subway to Hoyt–Schermerhorn Streets (A, C), to Atlantic Avenue–Barclays Center (D, N, R), or to Bergen Street (F, G) | Hours Mon–Fri 10am–10pm, Sat & Sun 9am–10pm | Tip Show off your ax-throwing skills at Kick Axe Throwing (622 Degraw Street, Brooklyn, NY 11217, www.kickaxe.com), a five-minute walk away in Gowanus.

55 _ Greenwood Park

A converted gas station is your new watering hole

The ingredients for a good bar are actually fairly simple: a nice variety of drinks, tasty fare to graze on, and a cozy atmosphere to linger in as twilight dissolves into darkness. Add in good music and a bit of entertainment to upgrade the rating to "excellent." Now, you've got the place you'll want to return to with your band of friends. A home away from home. But while the formula may be easy to articulate, it's much harder to achieve.

Greenwood Park, a 13,000-square-foot converted gas station and mechanic shop located in the netherland between Park Slope and Sunset Park manages to hit the mark where others fall short. With a street perimeter marked out with stacks of wooden pallets, the emphasis here is on comfy casual. The outdoor space is dominated by rows of picnic tables, perfect for a late-afternoon family rendezvous, especially during warmer months. A steady soundtrack of 80s' and 90s' rock keeps the atmosphere light and party-like. Loaded nachos and panko-crusted chicken fingers are perfect nibbles for the younger set, while parents enjoy Monday to Friday happy hours that run from noon to 7pm, with reductions on any of the more than two dozen beers on tap.

After 7pm, the ambience becomes strictly adult (21+ only). Share a pitcher of white or red sangria (or both), or relax with one of Greenwood Park's signature cocktails. Daddy's Little Helper (coffee-infused Jameson, cold brew coffee, and Irish cream) packs just the right pick-me-up punch, while the Greenwood Shandy (Schofferhofer Grapefruit Hefe, grapefruit vodka, and elderflower liqueur) offers a lighter, summery touch.

Cash only, ATMs are available to keep the drinks flowing. Kick back and watch the game on giant TV screens in both indoor and outdoor spaces, warmed by a fireplace and heat lamps on cool evenings. Or challenge your friends on one of three bocce courts late into the night.

Address 555 7th Avenue, Brooklyn, NY 11215, +1 (718)499-7999,
www.greenwoodparkbk.com, greenwoodparkbk@gmail.com | Getting there Subway
to 15th Street–Prospect Park (F, G) | Hours Mon–Thu & Sun noon–2am, Fri & Sat
noon–3am | Tip Enjoy bocce at public courts in Marine Park, Dyker Beach Park, and
McCarren Park, all available on a first come, first served basis. For a complete list of
courts, visit nycparks.gov/facilities/bocce, and click on the Brooklyn tab.

56_ Gristle Tattoo

Needles that relieve suffering

Combining an artistic impulse with public service, Gristle Tattoo perfectly straddles the twin poles of new Brooklyn's socially conscious, creative style. A vegan tattoo parlor that supports local animal shelters, Gristle has an underlying ethic of treating living things with compassion, whether it's a nervous, first-time tattoo recipient squirming in the chair or a scared kitten in need of a cozy home. That sense of mission originates among Gristle's warm and welcoming staff, and is underscored in their 100% vegan tattoo process. Then, there are those binders full of adoptable kitties you can browse while you're in the waiting area…

"Tattoos are our priority. We just happen to be vegan," owner Dina Dicenso clarifies, when asked to explain. "There are advantages to a vegan tattoo, even if you're not living a strictly vegan life." While tattoo ink is vegan, other parts of the process are not. "When people find out what's in their stuff, they care," she notes. Some inks, though not all, still have ingredients that are animal-derived. Stencil papers are commonly derived from lanolin. Disposable razors used in tattoo preparation often have that blue glycerine-based strip that contains animal-derived substances. Gristle also substitutes petroleum-based aftercare products like lotion with plant-based products.

Unlike rats in clinical trials, you sign a waiver before the tattoo artist applies needle to skin. Appointments are strongly encouraged, and deposits for work can be made through links on the website. But, despite the longtime association of tattoo artists with toughness and rebellion, Gristle is the embodiment of how these stereotypes are changing. Gristle's web presence makes it easy to participate in their pet adoption events with Whiskers-A-G-Go and RightMeowRescue, for example. Like much of hipster Brooklyn, the shop is a haven for people of diverse backgrounds looking for a refuge for free expression. This is anti-establishment cool – with a heart.

Address 26 Bushwick Avenue, Brooklyn, NY 11211, +1 (347)889-6422, www.gristletattoo.com, info@gristletattoo.com | **Getting there** Subway to Graham Avenue (L) | **Hours** To make an appointment, email info@gristletattoo.com | **Tip** Another local animal rescue is Badass Brooklyn. Look for adoption events and opportunities to foster dogs in need, as well as fun fundraisers, many involving dogs and drinks (www.badassbrooklyn.com).

57__Halva at Sahadi's
The bliss of that sweet, perfect crumble

If "Sahadi's halva" were in the dictionary, you might just find this definition: "a tasty treat that takes its name from a Yiddish word derived from a Turkish word with Arabic roots meaning 'sweet confection,' made by a grocer of Middle Eastern foods founded in Victorian Manhattan that's been a beloved Brooklyn institution for more than 65 years." That's it in a nutshell.

Originally from Lebanon, the Sahadi family opened a shop on Atlantic Avenue in 1948, landing in the middle of what was an historic Arab community that ran along the thoroughfare to the waterfront. Though the local real estate has transitioned and much of that community has since scattered, this grocer preserves a bit of that past. No mere historical anachronism, however, Sahadi's goods remain the borough's benchmark for ingredients by connoisseurs of Middle Eastern cuisine. The market's stellar reputation extends even to the national level, as it recently won a James Beard America's Classics Award as one of the country's top groceries. Ron Sahadi, co-owner and grandson of the founder of the Brooklyn store, sums it up, "We were artisanal before it was cool."

Each of Sahadi's halvas are produced locally by the same family for more than 50 years. The classic vanilla plain halva, suffused with the honied tastiness of crushed sesame combined with sugar and palm oil, can be eaten alone or, perhaps, blended into that bowl of ice cream you've saved for dessert. A second variety offers a slight variation courtesy of delicious pistachio bits. Finally, don't miss the marbled halva, whose flavor is supplemented with just the right amount of dark chocolate as well as almonds and cashews. While Sahadi's is the epicenter of halva in New York City, variations on this sweet treat can actually be found across the Middle Eastern diaspora throughout Africa, Asia, Europe, and the Americas. But no matter where you hale from, or what spelling variation you prefer, each bite is worth savoring.

Address 187 Atlantic Avenue, Brooklyn, NY 11201, +1 (718)624-4550, www.sahadis.com |
Getting there Subway to Borough Hall (2, 3, 4, 5) | Hours Mon–Sat 9am–7pm | Tip Since
the 1920s, Joyva, a company founded by Nathan Radutzky and named for his daughter –
you guessed it – Joy, has also been creating lovely halva and other luscious sweets in their
Brooklyn factory (www.joyva.com).

58__Handball Courts at Pier 2

Bouncing off the walls at Brooklyn Bridge Park

Playing handball at Pier 2 might just be like no other sporting experience you'll ever have. The water lapping at boulders that form the shoreline plays against the steady thrum of double-decker lanes of traffic on the BQE, above which sits a stately row of elegant Brooklyn Heights townhouses. As if that weren't enough, to the north, the iconic Brooklyn Bridge gracefully spans the East River, joining Brooklyn to a Manhattan that seems larger than life, behemoth glass towers shimmering in light. In the late afternoon, that light often migrates from pumpkin orange to blood red as the sun sets beyond Ellis Island and Lady Liberty. You can be forgiven if, with this feast of the senses all around, you occasionally lose track of the score.

Handball arrived in the borough via the wave of Irish immigrants who came over in the late 19th century. A one-wall version, the most popular outdoor variant of the game in Brooklyn, gradually evolved when beachgoers played against walls at Coney Island. Later, growth in the sport came when FDR's Works Progress Administration constructed courts throughout the city.

With over five acres of area, the six handball courts, covered for all-weather play, are only a portion of what's on offer at Pier 2. There are five full basketball courts (two covered), as are one bocce and three shuffleboard courts. A workout area offers fitness equipment, including specific ADA-approved pieces. There are swing sets and play areas for younger members of the sporty set, and picnic tables to take five and grab a drink. A roller rink, operated privately with skate rental available, is open at the water's edge. Free kayak use is available during the summer on a first come, first served basis. Kayak instruction is available for 11- to 18-year-olds, with a focus on safety. Space is limited, so check the website for details. Lockers are available for 25¢.

Address Pier 2, Brooklyn Bridge Park, Brooklyn, NY 11201, +1 (718)222-9939, www.brooklynbridgepark.org/park/pier-2 | **Getting there** Subway to High Street (A, C), to York Street (F), to Clark Street (2, 3), or to Court Street (R); ferry to DUMBO–Brooklyn Bridge Park Pier 1 (East River or South Brooklyn) | **Hours** Daily 6–11pm | **Tip** Handball courts abound throughout the borough. Check out the New York Park Department's website for locations (www.nycgovparks.org/facilities/handball, then click the Brooklyn tab).

59 Harbor Defense Museum

Letting objects tell the story of war

From the promontory of Fort Hamilton, a brief three-minute walk from the beautifully preserved Caponier that houses the Harbor Defense Museum, visitors to this hidden gem at Brooklyn's edge will have a spectacular up-close view of the Verrazano-Narrows Bridge. That view turns out to be important, as it provides the starting point for the story of why the fortress was built. The shoreline just beyond the streams of traffic on the Belt Parkway served, in late summer 1776, as the landing ground for the British troops that engaged Washington's colonial army in the Battle of Brooklyn. That conflict made the strategic importance of the Narrows, as the principal entrance to the city's harbor, absolutely clear.

When the War of 1812 reinforced this defensive need, Fort Hamilton was built. Though never under attack, it has stood ready to protect the harbor since its completion in 1831. One of a network of around 60 museums operated by the Department of Defense, director Justin Batt notes that the prime directive for each is to "stick to your story." Accordingly, the museum's collection of over 3,000 artifacts, many contributed by those who served here, have been astutely culled to distill this long and complex history. If available, one of the volunteer docents will provide rich texture to the materials on display.

From reproduction Revolutionary War uniforms and a Civil War-era Howitzer, to cannonballs and projectiles that highlight the evolution of ammunition, the exhibition traces the story of the American military in broad brushstrokes. For a more individual human touch, be sure not to miss the artifacts that tell the story of Gunner First Class Angelo Rizzo, a Brooklyn native who served in the Coastal Artillery Corps during World War I. Rizzo's diary allows us to follow the troop movements in France, culminating in 47 harrowing days of battle on the front at Argonne.

Address 230 Sheridan Loop, Brooklyn, NY 11252, +1 (718)630-4349, www.harbor-defense-museum.business.site | **Getting there** Subway to Bay Ridge–95 Street (R), take bus (B 8) to Fort Hamilton Parkway, then walk south along Fort Hamilton Parkway to the base entrance; parking is available | **Hours** Tue–Fri 10am–4pm | **Tip** Budget 15 to 20 extra minutes in order to be admitted to the US Army Garrison at Fort Hamilton. A photo ID is required, and you will need to complete an admission form at the base's Visitor's Center. If you choose to drive, you will also need to provide proof of insurance and registration.

60__Highest Subway Station
Taking "elevated" platforms to the extreme

It's difficult to think of the stop at Smith and 9th Streets as "sub" anything. Coming in a 87.5 feet *above* ground, the platforms for this stop on the F and G lines offer the fearful a chance to exchange claustro- for acrophobia.

Make a brief pitstop on your next ride to and from Prospect Park for distinctly different cityscapes. The platform sits above the Culver Viaduct, part of a mile-long stretch of track connecting Park Slope and Carroll Gardens. The Coney Island-bound platform offers, on its west end, an unobstructed view of lower Manhattan that shows off the city in all its audacious architectural might. This is Jay McInerney's *Bright Lights, Big City*, the playground of Tom Wolfe's "masters of the universe." Tall glassy towers that glimmer and gleam in the right sunlight dominate, though humanized by the carpet of building tops that fill the space between and the rattle and hum as the subway trains come and go. Pride of place goes to One World Trade Center, which stands in the place of the former Twin Towers, clocking in at 104 stories, or 1,776 feet tall – with its antenna.

Wander down to the east end of the same platform to peer down into the Gowanus Canal as it winds its way toward the sea and passes under the ever-bustling BQE. Still a working canal, and an EPA Superfund site being brought back to life by the efforts of locals, the waterway is what necessitated this passage of above-ground subway.

On the return trip, the City-bound platform offers a distinct set of perspectives. The eastern end looks out toward the Williamsburg Bank and the Atlantic Yards, being transformed daily through the rise of impressive skyscrapers rivalling those of Manhattan. Meanwhile, the west end offers a view out past the docks of Red Hook toward the harbor where, if the timing is right, you will enjoy a view of Lady Liberty bathed in gorgeous amber light.

Address The intersection of Smith Street and 9th Street, Brooklyn, NY 11231 | Getting there Subway to Smith Street–9th Street (F, G) | Hours Open 24 hours | Tip For another unique subway experience, make sure to visit Lorimer Street (J, M, Z) in Williamsburg. The open-air station features vibrant stained-glass window designs executed by artist Annette Davidek, and westbound trains offer iconic views of Manhattan from the Williamsburg Bridge.

61 Holocaust Memorial Park

Helping Brooklyn never to forget

Officially dedicated in June 1985, for more than 30 years, this park located near the water's edge in Sheepshead Bay has offered Brooklynites a place of quiet remembrance to reflect upon the murder of six million Jewish men, women, and children at the hands of the Nazis, and the other innocent five million victims of World War II. A central sculpture shows a beacon of light emerging from a partial crematorium chimney, the names of countries where these atrocities were committed carved on the base surround. Inscriptions along the base encapsulate this horrible history in stark, direct language.

On either side of the central structure, a number of granite stone markers resembling gravestones are engraved with the names of specific individuals martyred by the Nazis or memorialize sites where the exterminations occurred, the research organized by Holocaust scholar Monty Penkower. One marker tells the story of Bergen-Belsen and the death marches that added more than 37,000 deaths in the war's waning months, while another 28,000 died from medical complications following the British liberation of the camp. Another stone remembers victims from Wielun, Poland, bombed by the Luftwaffe in 1939 and whose one-third Jewish population was lost. Important figures, including Anne Frank, are honored, while the heroic efforts of Protestants from Le Chambon-sur-Lignon to hide and evacuate Jews are also remembered.

Hanan Simhon, vice president of the Holocaust Survivor Program of the organization, Self-Help, notes that approximately 25,000 survivors of the Holocaust still live in Brooklyn, most around 90 years of age and many in neighborhoods near the Memorial. "For many survivors," Simhon notes, "memories of their experiences were not openly discussed over their younger lives, as they were busy building new lives." This memorial captures some of those stories and makes certain that each new generation remembers this tragic history.

Address Holocaust Memorial Park, 66 West End Avenue, Brooklyn, NY 11235, +1 (646)801-0739, www.thmc.org, hmcorg@aol.com | **Getting there** Subway to Sheepshead Bay (Q) | **Hours** Unrestricted | **Tip** Varian Fry, a journalist whose rescue network helped save more than 2,000 anti-Nazi and Jewish refugees (including a who's who of artists and intellectuals), is buried in Green-Wood Cemetery (500 25th Street, Brooklyn, NY 11232, www.green-wood.com). Fry was the first American to be named "Righteous Among the Nations."

62__Homes of Creative Geniuses

Brooklyn Heights, where artistic lions roared

While most places would be content to have played home to one or two artistic titans, not so with Brooklyn Heights. Rambling among the charming tree-lined streets that capture the essence of refined, brownstone Brooklyn, it is possible within a matter of minutes to brush up against the homes and haunts of some of the greats of music, drama, and letters.

One house alone, at 7 Middagh Street (now demolished, but located below Willow Street near the playground), played home to a dozen or more. George Davis, fiction editor at *Harper's Bazaar* and later *Mademoiselle*, transformed a boarding house he rented for $75 a month into a bohemian artist commune, dubbed "February House" by visitor Anaïs Nin, due to the number of February birthdays. Residents included the authors Carson McCullers, Klaus Mann, and Richard Wright, poet W. H. Auden, composer Benjamin Britten and partner (British tenor) Peter Pears, authors Jane and Paul Bowles, and stripper Gypsy Rose Lee, who provided a house cook and maid in exchange for writing lessons from Davis.

A short walk away at 70 Willow Street, Truman Capote rented the basement apartment from his friend, Broadway set-designer Oliver Smith (*Oklahoma!*, *Porgy and Bess*). It was there that he worked on *Breakfast at Tiffany's* and *In Cold Blood* and famously wrote in his "A House in the Heights" essay, "I live in Brooklyn. By choice."

Farther along, at 5 Montague Terrace, novelist Thomas Wolfe lived in a pair of fourth-floor rooms while penning *Of Time and the River* (1933–35). Norman Mailer wrote his debut novel, *The Naked and the Dead*, from an attic studio at 20 Remsen Street. At Grace Court playwright Arthur Miller completed his masterpiece, *Death of a Salesman* (1949).

Address Various, see chapter for details | Getting there Subway to High Street (A or C), walk toward Brooklyn Bridge, turning left on Middagh Street. Walk to the end to see where "February House" once stood. | Hours Unrestricted from the outside only | Tip Poet Hart Crane gleaned inspiration for his epic poem, "The Bridge," while living at 110 Columbia Heights (now demolished). Ironically, he lived in the same room from which Brooklyn Bridge engineer Washington Roebling oversaw construction via a telescope from his window, while laying ill from the bends (see ch. 42).

63__House of Yes

Fusing art and the rave

Consider it a liberated zone. Anya Sapozhnikova and Kae Burke, New York City roommates from Rochester studying at the Fashion Institute of Technology, loved underground warehouse parties and Burning Man. But art school? Not so much. So, a plan was needed that would allow them to make art, have fun, and live the bohemian life they so desired. One thing led to another, and before they knew it, in 2007, they were taking over the lease of "a hippy-punk squat house complete with hallways filled with trash, leaky ceilings, and curious odors. Perfect, in other words," Anya said. "It's full of possibility," said Kae. The name, House of Yes, followed easily.

Renting rooms to a band of kindred spirits – performance artists, dancers, and musicians – the pair created, over time, a community of like-minded adventurers. Two venues and a decade later, the vision of creating a performance space open to all, celebrating the wild, wonderful, and weird, has been realized. The active calendar, curated by Anya and Kae, demonstrates the exciting genre-shifting range of offerings. One night might be a "Dirty Circus," combining drag, aerial acrobatics, and burlesque, while the next might be a themed DJ-driven dance party where attendees wear costumed attire. Still a third might be dominated by fire arts performers or a "Wondershow" combining magic and vaudeville. Programs like yoga or acoustic electronica offer the possibility to chill and connect with the cosmic, while another event is described as "a night of sin and skin and sacred play in the temple of pleasure." *Vive le difference!*

Be certain to check dress code info for your specific event under the "Ticket" tab on the website. Full service bars are on-site, and Queen of Falafel offers Middle Eastern food til 11pm most evenings. A generous outside patio is the place to grab a breath of the Bushwick night air.

Address 2 Wyckoff Avenue, Brooklyn, NY 11237, +1 (646)838-4937, www.houseofyes.org, info@houseofyes.org | Getting there Subway to Jefferson Street (L) | Hours See website for events schedule | Tip Roberta's New York Pizza is famous for their wood-fired pizza (261 Moore Street, Brooklyn, NY 11206, www.robertaspizza.com). It's also the home of Heritage Radio Network, broadcasting about all things food (www.heritageradionetwork.org).

64 IncrediPOLE

Body positivity

When the studio hosting a tight-knit pole-dancing community decided to shift gears, two of its members felt classes and the community were too important to disband. So Kirstin Dahmer and Sharon Goldberg set to work founding IncrediPOLE in an old Polish social club, not so much with the idea of serving as a replacement, but of creating a brand new community. "And, we have," Goldberg says with delight. "We've created a place that's all-welcoming for all-genders and all-body types – we're as open as we can possibly be. We just want to be a supportive and safe space where anyone can go."

That spirit of openness is obvious even in the Intro classes, which Goldberg describes as "Level Zero." "People always say they don't want to make a fool of themselves with other people in class who know what they are doing," she mentions sympathetically. "The Intro class is where everyone is a fool… It's really fun." For that first class, Goldberg suggests wearing something like shorts and a tank top. You'll need to be comfortable to move, and having some exposed skin is an asset, as it helps you grip the pole.

"Don't worry about being a success right away," Goldberg mentions, adding that the goal is to encourage self-acceptance. "You can just go through the motions of the class without exercising if you need to," she says, adding that "most people don't realize that just the smallest effort of showing up can be enough. We just want you to embrace yourself, and come try and hang out."

More advanced classes include techniques on either static or spinning poles (where the pole rotates based on body movements), and choreographing routines to music. The studio's Instagram feed features video clips of what you can expect to learn. "The bottom line is having fun," she says. "You're dancing and building muscle. To be strong is to be self-confident."

Address 145 Java Street, Suite 2R, Brooklyn, NY 11222, +1 (646)396-3699, www.incredipole.com | **Getting there** Subway to Greenpoint Avenue (G) | **Hours** Daily 11am–10pm; check the website for class schedules | **Tip** Make your daily life positive and healthy by visiting Green in BKLYN, a shop that makes living an eco-friendly lifestyle convenient and fun. Shop for green home and body products, as well as foods and items for children (432 Myrtle Avenue, Brooklyn, NY 11205, www.greeninbk.com).

65 Interference Archive

Get a hands-on view of protests of the past

Part repository, museum, exhibition space, and community discussion center, Interference Archive (IA) creates a space that welcomes both researchers and activists alike, and attempts to dissolve what can be arbitrary boundaries between them. Founded in 2011, IA originated from the personal accumulation of books, prints, and other ephemera gathered by Dara Greenwald and Josh MacPhee through their participation in a number of social movements and political art projects. With this material as a core, together with Molly Fair and Kevin Caplicki, the collection was organized into a wide-ranging archive that is preserving the kinds of items – buttons, posters, and leaflets, for example – that tend not to survive the causes that lead to their creation.

Louise Barry, one of more than 40 volunteers who staff IA, finds that the creation of the archive has actually been responsible for a consciousness about saving these often overlooked items. She notes, "Once people see that this collection exists, they say, 'Finally there is a place that I can take the posters I've saved over years of being involved, and I know that people will be able to see them.'" To date, IA has mounted more than 16 exhibitions concerning such diverse topics as the history of anti-nuclear movements, resistance movements against sexual violence, tenant organizing, and how social identity is expressed through comic art. They also host "propaganda parties" to distribute posters and materials for current protest events.

Perhaps IA's most distinctive feature is its open-access, open-stack policy. "Any visitor can take boxes off the shelves and look through them," Barry explains. "Usually, these kinds of items are in libraries where there are lots of restrictions. Our philosophy is 'preservation through use.' We preserve the ideas behind the materials by sharing the artifacts openly."

Address 314 7th Street, Brooklyn, NY 11215, www.interferencearchive.org, info@interferencearchive.org | **Getting there** Subway to 4 Avenue–9 Street (F, G, R) | **Hours** Thu noon–9pm, Fri, Sat, & Sun noon–5pm | **Tip** The Lesbian Herstory Archive (484 14th Street, Brooklyn, NY 11215, www.lesbianherstoryarchive.org) contains "the world's largest collection of materials by and about lesbians and their communities." Founded on a series of discussions in 1974, the archive has had a Park Slope home since 1993. The online calendar lists opening times for research and visiting.

66 Jalopy Theatre and School of Music

Come for the music, stay for the community

"It's called the Jalopy for a reason," co-founder Lynette Wiley notes. "We're not shiny and polished. We gamble that people will be open to our teachers' ideas. We're willing to say, 'Let's see what happens.'" Luckily, what often "happens" at Jalopy, both music school and performance space, is unique, even in a borough that prides itself on creativity and diversity.

Lynette and her husband Geoff arrived from Chicago in 2005 with the dream of creating a place where people of all ages, cultures, and abilities could feel at home. Classes and workshops are mostly in the early evenings or weekends. Kids programming (Jalopy Juniors) often ends with parents and children sharing a meal together. The stage becomes a place where musicians of many ethnic groups can interact. "Often, cultural groups only play for their own communities," Lynette adds. "We give them a chance to experience each other."

A month's worth of performances might feature Indian *raga*, Mexican *ranchera*, and African drumming and skiffle. Author and actor Sam Shepard used to occasionally perform in a jug band here. Spirit Family Reunion and Blind Boy Paxton have graced Jalopy's intimate stage. Classes, which have eight students maximum, are arranged in affordable eight-week sets, focusing on how to play particular instruments (guitar, fiddle, banjo, ukulele, and mandolin). No one is too inexperienced. Workshops on subjects like vocal harmony, slide guitar, or Balkan singing are also offered regularly. A small store has refurbished instruments for sale or rent.

"Put down your phone," Lynette says warmly. "Come in, experience something, be in a room with other people. Just that idea of being present and quiet is tonic, especially for New Yorkers. That's an education, too."

Address 315 Columbia Street, Brooklyn, NY 11231, +1 (718)395-3214, www.jalopytheatre.org |
Getting there Subway to Carroll Street (F, G) | Hours See website for class and performance
schedules | Tip Quilters and knitters may want to check out nearby Brooklyn General Store
(128 Union Street, Brooklyn, NY 11231, www.brooklyngeneral.com). The shop carries a great
collection of fabrics and hand-dyed wools and offers classes of all sorts.

67 Kings Theatre

Movie palace grandeur returns to Flatbush

A magnificent vaudeville and movie palace that formed part of a traveling MGM entertainment circuit in the New York City area, the Kings Theatre opened in Flatbush on September 7, 1929 as one of the original five Loew's "Wonder Theatres." Changing economic fortunes for the neighborhood brought gradual decay until, in 1977, the Kings was closed and abandoned. Left to the ravages of nature and looters, the Kings lay largely neglected until 2010, when Houston-based ACE Theatrical Group, LLC was chosen to lead what eventually became a $95-million restoration project. Vintage architectural elements, including ornate plaster moldings, pink marble staircases, and the sumptuous honeycomb ceiling, have been meticulously restored and recreated, and the original pipe organ console, removed and preserved during the closure by enthusiasts, is on display.

State-of-the-art stage and sound elements installed have transformed the Kings into a 3,200-seat theatrical and musical venue without peer. Largely still undiscovered by Manhattanites, the Kings offers intimate and smartly curated concerts that will satisfy baby boomers (The Temptations, The O'Jays), Gen Xers (Nick Cave and the Bad Seeds, The Pixies), and millennials (Sufjan Stevens, Bon Iver) alike. Historic "happy hour" tours offer visitors a chance to explore the Kings in more detail with a glass of wine in hand.

Just up the street, near Church Avenue, are two additional local landmarks. Erasmus Hall High School (899–925 Flatbush Avenue), founded in 1786, boasts a long list of notable alumni, including singers Neil Diamond and Barbra Streisand, actress Mae West, opera star Beverly Sills, and chess champion Bobby Fischer. Meanwhile, the Tiffany-studio stained-glass windows of Flatbush Dutch Reformed Church (890 Flatbush), founded in 1654, commemorate the many early Dutch families who worshipped there. The landmarked Art Deco Sears building sits just behind the Kings on Bedford Avenue.

Address 1027 Flatbush Avenue, Brooklyn, NY 11226, +1 (718)856-2220, www.kingstheatre.com, aceguestservices@theambassadors.com | Getting there Subway to Church Avenue (2, 5) | Hours See website for event and tour schedules | Tip Don't miss the original pipe organ on display just off the magnificent lobby. Removed and preserved during the closure by organ enthusiasts, it was returned to the Kings when it reopened in 2015.

68 Lefferts Historic House

Kids can imagine lives of farming and fighting

Built by Pieter Lefferts, a lieutenant in the Continental Army, in the years just after the Revolutionary War, this nicely preserved home of this old Brooklyn family now serves as a children's museum, focusing on life in Brooklyn circa 1820. Conveniently situated near Prospect Park's Children's Corner, the farmhouse can be readily combined with several other nearby attractions that together make for a wonderful day out for families with small children.

Home to one of the wealthiest landowning families in Brooklyn, Pieter was descended from Leffert Pietersen Van Haughwout, one of the original Dutch families who arrived in 1660 to farm a sparsely populated Brooklyn. His house, built in 1680 a few blocks away near the intersection of Flatbush Avenue and Maple Street, was burned by American troops in 1776, just prior to the Battle of Brooklyn to prevent British troops from using it as a foothold. After the war, a new house (the current one) was built in the same location, where members of the family lived until 1915. No longer farmers, they divided the land into 600 parcels (now the basis of the Prospect-Lefferts Garden neighborhood), and the house was moved to this location.

Lefferts amassed some 240 acres of central borough farmland, and his household included 12 slaves. Several of the rooms now are decorated with period furniture, and board displays contain pictures and info aimed at providing an understanding of early 19th-century family life, including slavery, not outlawed in New York state until 1827. Outside, a small garden and the remains of the kitchen provide a chance for smaller children to explore and play.

Steps away you'll find both an entrance to the Prospect Park Zoo, which features 12-acres' worth of kid-friendly animal encounters, and an historic carousel. Crafted in 1912 and lovingly restored in 1990, the team of 53 horses are irresistible!

Address 452 Flatbush Avenue, Brooklyn, NY 11225, +1 (718)965-8951, www.prospectpark.org/visit-the-park/places-to-go/lefferts-historic-house, info@prospectpark.org | Getting there Subway to Prospect Place (B, Q, S) | Hours Thu – Sun & holidays noon – 5pm | Tip Make sure to look for the small octagonal structure near the Lefferts House. This is the only toll booth remaining from a wood-planked road that followed Flatbush from where the Atlantic Terminal is to the Dutch Reformed Church (890 Flatbush Avenue, Brooklyn, NY 11226), and in which Lefferts was an investor.

69 Literary Doors

A novel idea at the Brooklyn Public Library

Standing on the front steps of the Brooklyn Public Library and looking toward Grand Army Plaza, it's difficult not to feel like a master of the universe. Before you, amid the swirl of traffic, stands the Soldiers' and Sailors' Arch. To the left is the road leading into the magnificent Prospect Park. Eastern Parkway takes you to the Brooklyn Museum of Art and Brooklyn Botanic Garden. Turning, you find Brooklyn's temple of knowledge, the Central Branch of the Public Library.

If you were able to look down from above, you would notice that the building takes the shape of an open book. Groundbreaking for the original building was in 1912, but financial hardship created by World War I and the Great Depression, cost overruns, and political quarrels saw construction grind to a halt, incomplete. Work finally resumed in 1935 but with the Beaux Arts features eliminated; thus the stark, somewhat sober façade.

That is, except for the doors that make up the library's entrance. Positioned within the 50-foot-tall portico, and between two gilded limestones columns celebrating science and the arts, the bronze doors feature 15 panels that might best be described as literary hieroglyphs. Like a puzzle, each pictograph celebrates characters and authors from American literature. How many can you identify? Beginning at the top and reading left to right, they are: Hester Prynne of *The Scarlet Letter*, Archy and Mehitabel from humorist Don Marquis' stories, and Meg from *Little Women*; Babe the Blue Ox from *Paul Bunyon*, Longfellow's *Hiawatha*, and Jack London's *White Fang*; Washington Irving's *Rip van Winkle*, Joel Chandler's *Brer Rabbit*, and James Fenimore Cooper's Natty Bumppo; Melville's *Moby Dick*, poet Walt Whitman, and Edgar Allen Poe's raven; and Mark Twain's *Tom Sawyer*, Eugene Field's *Wynken, Blynken, and Nod*; and Richard Henry Dana, Jr., author of *Two Years Before the Mast*.

Address 10 Grand Army Plaza, Brooklyn, NY 11238, +1 (718)230-2100, www.bklynlibrary.org/locations/central | **Getting there** Subway to Grand Army Plaza or Eastern Parkway/Brooklyn Museum (2, 3) | **Hours** Unrestricted view of the doors; see website for library hours | **Tip** Across from the Library, get a closer look at Soldiers' and Sailors' Arch, commemorating the "Defenders of the Union," Northern troops in the Civil War (www.nycgovparks.org/parks/grand-army-plaza/monuments/1463).

70 _Masstransiscope

Let your subway car take you to the exhibition

Commuters facing forward while departing on Manhattan-bound B or Q trains from Dekalb Avenue look sharply to the right and keep their fingers crossed that the train keeps moving at a normal clip. The reason? These conditions make for ideal viewing of one of the city's most frequently viewed works of art. The *Masstransiscope* takes its inspiration from the zoetrope, a Victorian-era animation device that consisted of a set of individual drawings pasted to the inside wall of a spinning cylinder, illuminated but behind screens, viewable through vertical slits. With the train providing the motion, 228 separate panels painted over a distance of 300 feet on the walls of an abandoned subway tunnel simulate an animated scene about 20 seconds in length.

Colorful and playful, the work was created in 1980 by artist Bill Brand, whose films have been shown in festivals internationally. Supported by the art organization Creative Time and the MTA, this original work was well-received. But it eventually fell into disrepair and lay dormant and largely unseen for most of the next 20 years. (Brand has spoken about sneaking into the station during the 1980s to clean and repair the work himself!) Then, in 2008, the work was revived and restored, and it was repaired yet again when it was vandalized following Hurricane Sandy. Closing in on 40 years old, Brand's work is still a delightful interlude during what can be an otherwise tedious commute.

Engaging works are sprinkled throughout the subway system, courtesy of MTA Arts and Design commissions since 1985. Check out Stephen T. Johnson's *Dekalb Improvisation*, a lively collage that incorporates the Brooklyn Bridge. Look for the futuristic stained-glass designs of Ellsworth Ausby's *A Space Odyssey* at Marcy Avenue. And ponder the homes seen from the elevated trains with Eugenie Tung's *16 Windows* at New Utrecht Avenue station.

Address Manhattan-bound D and Q subways between Dekalb Avenue and Flatbush Avenue Stations, www.billbrand.net/about.masstransiscope.html | Getting there Subway Manhattan-bound (B, Q) through Dekalb Avenue station | Hours Unrestricted from the subway | Tip Subway art pays tribute to architecture at the 2 and 3 train's Eastern Parkway/ Brooklyn Museum stop. Each piece incorporates an ornamental artifact salvaged from a former building. There are 78 pieces in all, viewable at the station's mezzanine level. For details on this and other pieces of subway art, visit the guide at www.nycsubway.org.

71 Misses Brooklyn and Manhattan

A pair of statuesque beauties welcoming all

Banished when urban-planning czar Robert Moses judged them too much of a distraction for drivers (despite the fact they had been in position for nearly half a century by that point), this pair of figures representing Brooklyn and Manhattan sit together once again at the base of the Manhattan Bridge, welcoming – or is it bidding adieu? – travellers headed up and down Flatbush Avenue. The original statues, carved in granite by sculptor Daniel Chester French, who most famously sculpted Abraham Lincoln for his memorial in Washington, D.C., were commissioned in 1913 to celebrate the joining of the boroughs by the bridge after it opened in 1909. Positioned on pylons near the Brooklyn end of the span, the couple reigned until 1963, when shifting traffic patterns led to their removal. The pair eventually found their way to the Brooklyn Museum, where they are displayed somewhat less prominently above the spaceship-like entrance added to the façade in 2003 on Eastern Parkway.

In late December 2016, replicas of the allegorical duo returned, the result of a decade-long process sponsored by the Economic Development Corporation and One Percent for Art. Cast in lighter, resilient acrylic resin by sculptor Brian Tolle, whose *Irish Hunger Memorial* (2002) can be viewed in Battery Park, Miss Manhattan sits stately and erect, gazing out onto some unseen horizon, her foot resting upon a chest of treasures, her left hand grasping an orb. Meanwhile, Miss Brooklyn enjoys a more relaxed pose, clutching a tablet, a child with its head buried in a book at her feet. The message still reads crystal clear: one is the image of haughty swagger, the other of self-confident cool.

Illuminated from within by LED lighting at night, the pair rest atop a 30-foot steel structure reminiscent of a lamp post, each sitting on its own rotating disc. Finally, a worthy distraction while sitting in traffic!

Address Flatbush Avenue Extension and Tillary Street, Brooklyn, NY 11201 | Getting there Subway to Dekalb Avenue (B, Q) | Hours Unrestricted | Tip From here, head over to nearby MetroTech Commons, the heart of downtown Brooklyn's business development area. The central square, found between Lawrence and Duffield Streets, often hosts outdoor art and sculpture exhibitions (www.downtownbrooklyn.com/listings/metrotech-commons).

72__Moore Brothers
Wine Co.
Taste the difference

If you don't know as much about wine as you'd like, the key is to have that one special wine shop, where you have a relationship with the staff and trust their recommendations. Now, imagine you had a wine shop where the owners also had that kind of special personal relationship with each of the producers whose wines line the shelves. Moore Brothers offers customers precisely that kind of knowledge base and experience. Store manager Ecco Adler notes, "We go to the vineyards and examine each part of the process. Over the years, we've developed personal relations based on trust with our winemakers and our customers."

Forged over the course of more than 25 years, those personal relationships are the intangible special ingredient in every bottle. "Our producers are small vineyards committed to environmental sustainability, to the sustainability of their cultures," Adler notes. "In many cases, these are vineyards that have been in families over several generations." Moore Brothers is definitely doing their part to preserve these small, high-quality operations, and the relationship is well worth the effort. "We do our part to take care of their work. We ship the wines at a constant temperature, the same temperature they are stored at in the shop. This makes sure they arrive at your table just the way they were meant to be."

Brothers Greg and David Moore bring several decades of experience pairing wine with foods as well to help you curate your next dinner party with sophistication and flair. Adler estimates that about 75 vineyards are currently represented in the shop. While the majority are from France, Germany, and Italy, a few choice selections from Argentina and California mean New World partisans will leave satisfied as well. Three or four bottles are almost always open to sample, and Moore Brothers also delivers with great care.

Address Industry City, 51 35th Street, Brooklyn, NY 11232, +1 (844)305-5023, www.store.moorebrothers.com | Getting there Subway to 36 Street (D, N, R) | Hours Mon–Fri 11am–8pm, Sat 10am–6pm, Sun noon–5pm | Tip Leave plenty of time to explore the other inhabitants of the Industry City complex (www.industrycity.com), a 16-building complex that sits alongside the BQE in Sunset Park. Be sure to try Japan Village, a 20,000-square-foot food hall that offers the best in Asian cuisine.

73 Murder Inc. Headquarters
The mob's little shop of horrors

Sitting in the shadow of the elevated tracks of the 3 train, this un-assuming Brownsville bodega looks more like a place to pick up a newspaper than one of the most notorious centers of criminal operations in New York City mob history. But in the 1930s, the corner shop, then Midnight Rose's Candy Store, served as headquarters for the National Crime Syndicate's enforcement arm. Though the exact number of victims "sleeping with the fishes" will never be known, the group, which came to be known as Murder Incorporated for its business-like approach to contract killing, is thought to be responsible for somewhere between 400 to 1,000 murders.

Established in the aftermath of a bloody gang war for control of the American mafia, Murder Inc. was headed by Louis "Lepke" Bechalter and later Albert "Mad Hatter" Anastasia as a "Chinese Wall" to protect *Cosa Nostra* bosses from the legal consequences of their crimes. Killing orders would be passed through conduits to local mobsters from the Jewish Brownsville Boys and the Italian Ocean Hill Hooligans who had no direct connections to the victims. One member, Harry "Pittsburgh Phil" Strauss, was particularly prolific – and creative – killing more than 100 (some say 500) through means that included shooting, strangulation, ice pick, and even live burial.

Eventually, the ring was brought down when Abe "Kid Twist" Reles, one of the group's most feared hitmen, got caught by the police, turned state's evidence and sent several of his fellow Murder Inc. assassins to the electric chair. Set to testify against Anastasia, Reles "accidentally fell out of a window" while in police custody at the Half Moon Hotel in Coney Island. Meanwhile, Midnight Rose feigned innocence about the whole affair. Asked by police why she let these thugs into her candy store, she supposedly retorted, "Why don't the police keep them out?"

Address 779 Saratoga Avenue, Brooklyn, NY 11212 | Getting there Subway to Saratoga Avenue (3); the site is under the elevated tracks at the intersection with Livonia Avenue | Hours Unrestricted from the outside only | Tip Murder Inc. boss Albert Anastasia, also known as "Lord High Executioner," led what eventually became the Gambino crime family. Entering the country illegally from a freight ship on which he and his brothers were working, he first worked as a Brooklyn longshoreman and lived in Red Hook (126 Pioneer Street, Brooklyn, NY 11231). Anastasia is buried in Green-Wood Cemetery.

74_ The Muse Brooklyn

Come here before you run away and join the circus

"I think a lot of people are genuinely intimidated by starting something like circus," says Angela Buccinni Butch, founder and director of this Bushwick-based school for circus arts. "It's definitely a very athletic form, and sometimes people come in thinking they don't have the right body strength." Her answer is a simple one: "Of course you don't. You've just started!"

Offering classes in a host of traditional disciplines, including aerial acrobatics, tumbling, juggling, wheeled apparatuses, and contortion, the Muse's small class size allows the emphasis to be on personalized instruction and safety. While some participants are training for careers in circus performance, Buccinni Butch emphasizes that everyone is welcome and that many of their classes focus on introductory level skills. "We have really great teachers who can provide foundation-level building blocks. From there it is amazing to see what is possible." Children's classes are also offered and, on weekends, the Muse throws open its doors to families for donation-based free play, where a safe space is set up for parents and children to explore. She also encourages would-be participants to come observe a class (though she checks in with teachers and students first).

The Muse's airy, open space means that it is not unusual to see students grappling with silks or lyra (an aerial hoop), flying on a trapeze, and finding balance on a unicycle all at once. Exciting to be sure, but for those new to circus, the splendor of it all can arouse a world of doubt. But, bit by bit, the hard work can conquer lingering doubt. "One of my favorite things is noticing how much people's minds change over the course of time, and seeing, after a little work, people achieve something they thought was impossible," Buccinni Butler reflects. "The circus has the power to change people's minds."

Address 350 Moffat Street, Brooklyn, NY 11237, +1 (929)400-1678, www.themusebrooklyn.com | **Getting there** Subway to Wilson Avenue (L), parking also available | **Hours** See website for class schedules | **Tip** The Muse's new Gowanus location (303 3rd Avenue, Brooklyn, NY 11215, www.themusegowanus.com) puts the focus on children and families with specially designed classes.

75__National Sawdust

A former factory builds an audience for new music

There's something boundary-defying about placing an artistic venue inside the reconfigured space of a former sawdust processing factory, something that equates and dignifies creative processes with the imprimatur of labor. Taking the factory's name merely underscores that essence. It reminds those who attend performances here of their privilege in doing so, that the spectacle around them occurs in a place with a peopled history whose spirits linger, that this factory is a sacred space.

Defining itself as a place for "exploration and discovery," National Sawdust attempts to meet that goal with an ambitious calendar of music, theater, and dance. Whether in a series of concerts specially curated by master artists or a group listening party for a classic rock album, the focus is on disrupting normal ways of hearing, of challenging the audience to rethink *how* to listen. A set of conversations with distinguished creators and thinkers provide the medium for much of this perceptual deconstruction.

Special focus is put on emerging artists. As an incubator for new work and talent, the organization gives composers and musicians resources and the luxury of time and space to develop their art. Past artists-in-residence have included the innovative string quartet Brooklyn Rider, photographer-filmmaker Murat Euyboglu, and rising opera mezzo-soprano Eve Gigliotti. National Sawdust also provides support for project development and realization. In the past, for example, they assisted composer-performer Julia Holter in her development of an opera based on *Euripedes*; composer Huang Ruo in work on his multidimensional audience-interactive work; and composer-instrumentalist Angélica Negrón in the creation of a new chamber opera that features seven drag performers.

Rider, the in-house restaurant, was created by James Beard Award-winning chef Patrick Connolly.

Address 80 North 6th Street, Brooklyn, NY 11249, +1 (646)779-8455, www.nationalsawdust.org, info@nationalsawdust.org | Getting there Subway to Bedford Avenue (L) | Hours Mon–Fri 10–1am, Sat & Sun noon–11pm | Tip For innovative theater offerings, check out Third Rail Projects (697 Grand Street, PMB 126, Brooklyn, NY 11211, www.thirdrailprojects.com), whose work includes *Then She Fell*, an immersive theater experience based upon Lewis Carroll's *Alice in Wonderland*.

76__New World's First Landlady

Here is the birthplace of women's equality

More than a century before the Bill of Rights, religious freedom took center stage in the town charter of this Brooklyn outpost founded by Lady Deborah Moody (c.1583–1649). Born into an established English family, Deborah became Lady Moody when her husband Henry was knighted by James I in 1606. Widowed, then brought before the Star Chamber for her unconventional Anabaptist beliefs (namely, that children should not be baptized), Lady Moody sold her estate and migrated at age 54 to colonial Massachusetts, where she knew John Winthrop and hoped to escape persecution. But Moody wasn't accepted there either. Within four years, she was excommunicated by church leaders. Branded "a Dangerous woeman" by the deputy-governor, the rebellious Moody relocated with fellow believers first to New Amsterdam, then (when problems continued) to a patch of swampy marshland given by Dutch Governor Willem Kieft.

Granted a tract of 7,000 acres, Lady Moody established Gravesend, the first colony in the New World established by a woman. Moody's village embraced religious tolerance from the start, even inviting a group of Quakers expelled by the Dutch to settle in the community when they were chased out of New Amsterdam by Governor Peter Stuyvesant.

A planned community, the footprint of Moody's original design remains in place. MacDonald Avenue forms the north-south axis, while Gravesend Neck Road runs east to west. Van Sicklen House (27 Gravesend Neck Road), Brooklyn's only surviving Dutch home of stone construction, marks the site of Lady Moody's original home, though the current structure dates much later from the 18th century. Directly across the street is Old Gravesend Cemetery, created in 1643 (not open to the public). Legend has it that Lady Moody was buried there when she died in 1659, though her grave is unmarked.

GRAVESEND WAS FOUNDED IN 1643

BY LADY DEBORAH MOODY

WHO NAMED THIS COMMUNITY

AFTER HER HOME TOWN GRAVESEND,

ENGLAND, FOUNDED ON THE PRECEPTS OF

RELIGIOUS FREEDOM. GRAVESEND,

WHICH MEANS

AT THE END OF THE GROVE,

DERIVES ITS NAME FROM

TWO SAXON WORDS

"GRAFES ENDE"

OCT. 4, 1987
GRAVESEND
TIME CAPSULE
CONTAINING THE HISTORY
IS LOCATED 22 ND AND
DUE WEST OF THIS
MEMORIAL

Address Lady Moody Triangle, Avenue U, Brooklyn, NY 11223, www.nycgovparks.org/parks/lady-moody-triangle/history | **Getting there** Subway to Avenue U (F, N) | **Hours** Unrestricted from the outside only | **Tip** Visit Nuccio's nearby (261 Avenue U, Brooklyn, NY 11223, www.nucciosbakery.com), a traditional Italian bakery that sits opposite Lady Moody Triangle, for a cannoli or a fresh fruit tart.

77 Newtown Creek Nature Walk

A small park that asks a big question

Imagine this park as a cathedral to nature, to Newtown Creek, to the present, and to what used to be. Like a master builder from the Middle Ages erecting a structure encoded with words and symbols meant to inspire and inform, environmental sculptor George Trakas has designed this largely unknown park in an obscure, industrial corner of Greenpoint with elements that, with a little imagination, educate visitors about aspects of the life here from the time of the indigenous Lenape people to the present day.

Find your way to the intersection of Provost Street and Paidge Avenue and pause for a moment at a pair of large stones near the corner, both from the last Ice Age, some 17,000 years ago. A small column of trees – sweet gums, red oaks, and honey locusts, all specially chosen as native varieties – guide you toward the entrance. Arriving at a gate, follow a small rocky path underneath the bridge to a small planting of fragrant plants before continuing on. Here, Trakas reminds visitors that this area hosted the shipbuilding industry during the 19th century: the walkway walls are formed like ship planks and contain portholes to peer through, now onto this post-industrial terrain.

Following the pathway as it bends toward Newtown Creek, you also begin to see elements of the Manhattan skyline. Make your way to Seven Stone Circle, where Trakas has positioned sculpted flat rings, each engraved with Lenape place names of areas oriented in that direction. The water gently laps upon steps here at *Mespaethes*, "the great brook with tide," an excellent site from which to consider the environmental impact of four centuries of urbanization. The area was once one of the most polluted sites in the US, containing some 30 million gallons of toxic waste. Nearby, a 1,400-lb. granite table with an etched map of the original watershed begs us to ask, "What brought us here?"

Address Provost Street and Paidge Avenue, Brooklyn, NY 11222, www.nyc.gov/html/dep/html/environmental_education/newtown.shtml | Getting there Subway to Greenpoint Avenue (G) | Hours Daily dawn–dusk, weather permitting | Tip To become a part of reclaiming another EPA Superfund site, volunteer with the Gowanus Canal Conservancy (www.gowanuscanalconservancy.org) in efforts like tree planting, weeding, compost sifting, and many other useful care and maintenance activities.

78_Niblo's Garden

Dancing around their graves

After complaints of smells coming from Trinity Cemetery in Manhattan, Green-Wood Cemetery was created in 1838 as a rural alternative. An early version of a public park, it became a popular attraction for Victorian New Yorkers, drawing half a million visitors a year to wander its tree-lined paths. (Its popularity served as a main rationale for the later construction of Central Park.) Modeled on Paris' Père Lachaise Cemetery, Green-Wood's owners marketed it as the elite address for the afterlife. The free map at the entrance will help you find the final resting places of celebrated artists Jean-Michel Basquiat and Louis Comfort Tiffany; "West Side Story" composer Leonard Bernstein and "New York, New York" lyricist Fred Ebbs; and presidential candidates Horace Greeley and DeWitt Clinton. Notorious Tammany Hall politician "Boss" Tweed, who stole $200 million from city coffers, is here with mob boss Anastasio Umberto, leader of the enforcement gang known as Murder Inc., reportedly responsible for some 400 murders (see ch. 73), as well as "Crazy Joe" Gallo, the "little guy with steel balls" who killed him in a barber's chair.

There are countless stories behind the tombs at Green-Wood. Perhaps none is more peculiar than that of William Niblo. An immigrant from Ireland, Niblo opened the Bank Coffee House near New York's financial center that became *the* place for the New York "it" crowd to see and be seen. He then opened the wildly successful Niblo's Garden, an open-air tavern that staged performances by lantern light, including PT Barnum's first spectacular.

Heartbroken when his wife Martha died in 1851, Niblo built a large mausoleum near the cemetery's picturesque Crescent Waters. For 27 years until his death, he visited her tomb almost every day, often bringing friends along for parties and picnics, a practice Green-Wood now celebrates with an annual summer soirée, featuring performers from the Bindlestiff Family Cirkus.

Address 500 25th Street, Brooklyn, NY 11232, +1 (718)210-3080, www.green-wood.com, events@green-wood.com | Getting there Subway to 25 Street (R) | Hours See website for hours, which vary for each entrance and season | Tip Across the street from the cemetery entrance, enjoy a coffee and take home a fresh loaf of bread from Baked in Brooklyn (755 5th Avenue, New York, NY 10022, www.bakedinbrooklynny.com). You can watch the bakers at work through the windows as you wait.

79_ Olly OxenFree Vintage

Breathe new life into your old wardrobe

Olly OxenFree Vintage is a sanctuary for fashion of bygone eras. The vintage store has been open since 2012 but feels like it has been setting trends for decades. The shop has a clear love for fashion and design from the 40s through 70s with coats, kimonos, cocktail dresses, vintage tees, and full-on costumes, all carefully curated and cataloged in visually stunning ways by Suzy, the store's owner and founder.

It is easy to get lost among the beautiful fabrics and patterns that swaddle you when you first step inside the space from the bustling sidewalk. There is not a warmer and cozier place in Brooklyn. Suzy decks out every inch of her space to provide a little universe lost in time. She encourages patrons to try on one-of-a-kind pieces that she personally hand selects with care. You can't help but want to touch and get to know each piece of clothing and learn their stories. Suzy is knowledgeable and is more than willing and able to help visitors find pieces for events, projects, or personal collections. Open since 2012, this is the one-stop clothing oasis of your dreams.

Fundraisers and events are always percolating at Olly OxenFree. In the front you might find vintage tees that Suzy worked with artists to adorn with "No DAPL" (No Dakota Access Pipeline), with proceeds supporting the cause. The back of the store has held fundraisers and benefit concerts for Planned Parenthood and Standing Rock, among others. Along with political and social events, Olly OxenFree hosts classes, music events, and readings. Every Sunday the space in the back is opened up for a first-come, first-served yoga class taught by an accredited yoga teacher well versed in tantra and kundalini yoga, who teaches in the city at a top studio but comes once a week for a donation-based class at Olly OxenFree Vintage. This store is a must-visit, as it combines the magic of your big sister's closet and the historical interest of a museum.

Address 137 Montrose Avenue, Brooklyn, NY 11206, +1 (347)762-5048, www.ollyoxenfreevintage.com, oofvintage@gmail.com | **Getting there** Subway to Montrose Avenue (L) | **Hours** Mon, Wed, Thu 11am–8pm, Fri–Sun 11am–7pm | **Tip** Antoinette (119 Grand Street, Brooklyn, NY 11249, www.antoinettebrooklyn.com) offers a balance of old and new on its racks. Roughly 70% of their clothing stock is vintage, while 30% is the work of Brooklyn-based designers.

80__ Ovenly
Brooklyn blackout cake for the 21st century

Ebinger's, Brooklyn's legendary bakery founded in 1898 by German immigrant Arthur Ebinger, has almost mythical status among old timers. By the time the company shuttered in 1972, there were 58 shops, and the brand was the gold standard in freshly baked cakes and pastries. Ah, but time marches on: the brand's overexpansion onto Long Island led to a bankruptcy that sent the borough into mourning. Suddenly, Ebinger's tasty treats were no more, with no loss felt more heavily than the beloved "blackout cake." A sweet tooth's pure delight, the cake included several layers of moist chocolate cake separated by chocolate cream, topped off with chocolate icing and – surprise, surprise – chocolate crumbs from the cake itself. The name came from the "blackout" drills that were routine during World War II to protect the nearby Navy Yard, though it might just as easily have been the diabetic coma you might well fall into after a few rich forkfuls.

Fast forward to 2010 when Erin Patinkin and Agatha Kulaga launched Ovenly. Having met in a food-themed book club, the only two non-food professionals (Erin worked with nonprofits, and Agatha was doing psychiatric research) teamed up to start a business making baked goods. Drawing upon Brooklyn's past, one of the delectable cakes Ovenly created was a reimagining of Ebinger's signature item. Moist, soft, and definitely black, the updated version relies on a pair of innovations: dark cocoa powder, which insures the color and imparts a taste of bittersweet, and Brooklyn Brewery's Black Chocolate Stout, which provides a hearty chocolatey and malty character. Less on the nose than its historical forebear, this is a sophisticated adventure.

Another reason to love Ovenly? In partnership with two nonprofits, the bakery offers a training program that promotes hiring for diversity, including both formerly incarcerated individuals and refugees.

Address 31 Greenpoint Avenue, Brooklyn, NY 11222, +1 (888)899-2213, www.oven.ly, info@oven.ly | *Getting there* Subway to Greenpoint Avenue (G) | *Hours* Mon–Fri 7:30am–7pm, Sat & Sun 8am–7pm | *Tip* Enjoy your treats down the block at WNYC Transmitter Park (Greenpoint Avenue, Brooklyn, NY 11222, www.nycgovparks.org/parks/transmitter-park). Formerly the site of the local public radio station's transmitter tower, the space was converted to a beautiful waterside park in 2012 and features stunning views of the Manhattan skyline.

81 — Park Slope Plane Crash
The nightmare before Christmas

The morning of December 16, 1960 was an ordinary, pre-holiday Friday. Anxious shoppers were several days away from Christmas, and there would be four candles to light in the menorah that evening. Two weeks before, the musical *Camelot* debuted on Broadway, and a mere five weeks remained before a new administration that some would later call Camelot arrived in Washington.

Meanwhile, events in the skies above New Jersey were about to change this peacefulness. United Airlines Flight 826, originating at Chicago's O'Hare Airport and carrying 77 passengers and 7 crew, notified company flight operators that part of its navigational system was not operating properly. However, air traffic control was not notified of this problem. So when the flight's landing path to Idlewild Airport (now JFK) was revised, the plane flew off-course, intersecting the path of TWA flight 266, originating in Dayton and carrying 39 passengers and 5 crew, on its way to LaGuardia Airport. The TWA 266 plane split apart and spiraled into a field on Staten Island, while United 826 glided on, eventually crashing down just shy of Prospect Park at the corner of Sterling Place and Seventh Avenue, killing almost everyone on board and six people on the ground as well.

Eleven-year-old Stephen Baltz, flying alone to meet up with his family, was thrown from the fuselage and landed in a snowbank. Alive and conscious, the young boy was rushed to New York-Presbyterian Brooklyn Methodist Hospital and was able to tell his rescuers about looking out the window as the plane plummeted: "It looked like a picture in a fairy book. It was a beautiful sight." Sadly, Stephen died the next day of pneumonia from inhaling the burning jet fuel. Little evidence of the horrific crash remains, but at the top of 126 Sterling Place, you can see the brickwork that was replaced after the plane's wing destroyed the original section.

Address Intersection of Sterling Place and Seventh Avenue, Brooklyn, NY 11217 | **Getting there** Subway to 7 Avenue (B, Q) | **Hours** Unrestricted | **Tip** Young Stephen Baltz is honored with a small plaque located in the chapel of NewYork-Presbyterian Brooklyn Methodist Hospital (506 Sixth Street, Brooklyn, NY 11215, www.nyp.org/brooklyn). Change found in the young boy's pockets is embedded in the panel.

82 — Pioneer Works

A cultural center for the whole community

The air at Pioneer Works in Red Hook buzzes like it's alive, as if the enormous interior still resonates from its iron-works-factory past. Now, thanks to a dedicated community guided by the vision of director and founder Dustin Yellin, the repurposed expanse incubates a creative community. Sheetal Prajapati, Pioneer's director of public engagement, describes their space as "a multidisciplinary cultural center where art, tech, music, and education coexist." Housing two recording studios, six artist studios, several 3-D printers, and a huge performance venue that always has something unique and engaging going on, Pioneer Works is an establishment built by artists for artists that knows how essential art-appreciating visitors and music lovers are with that equation.

Tucked discreetly among a warren of warehouses and just a stone's throw away from Governor's Island, Pioneer Works is an unassuming building that, apart from its size, doesn't really stand out from the buildings that surround. An essential part of the Red Hook cityscape and a short walk from local Red Hook fare, Pioneer Works is as much a part of the neighborhood as the people who live there and the bars, pizza shops, and gelato spots that line the adjacent streets.

Shortly after the venue opened in 2012, Hurricane Sandy devastated Red Hook. This tragedy gave the people of Pioneer Works a new sense of purpose and dedication to community outreach and support. Today, Pioneer Works facilitates classes and events for local organizations, teaming up with after-school programs via the Red Hook Initiative and the Vera List Center for Art and Politics. In 2017, Pioneer Works put their space to use by hosting the first city council debate for their district. Pioneer Works takes its role as a community sounding board seriously and strongly identifies as "In Red Hook, and about Red Hook." Be sure not to miss Second Sunday, a monthly free event featuring programs and open studios.

Address 159 Pioneer Street, Brooklyn, NY 11231, +1 (718)596-3001, www.pioneerworks.org | **Getting there** Subway to Smith Street–9th Street (F, G), then take bus B 61 to King Street | **Hours** See website for schedule | **Tip** Take a tour of Red Hook's Widow Jane Distillery & Cacao Prieto Chocolate Factory, which produces "bean-to-bar chocolate made fresh daily from the finest organic, single origin Dominican Cacao and distills a line of small batch, cacao-based liqueurs and rums." Yes, please (218 Conover Street, Brooklyn, NY 11231, www.widowjane.com).

83__Please

An educated pleasure shop

That Please aspires to be something different is obvious from the start. The shop's glass front screams that this is definitely *not* your parents' sex shop, although owner Sid Azmi makes almost no assumptions about what our parents get up to. "I want to bring sex out into the open, to make it something that people of any age can talk about," she says without a hint of a whisper. "No stigma and no shame. Sex is on everybody's mind, though everyone's afraid to talk about it. But, once you say the word, it's like opening a Pandora's box. Discussion flows."

Please offers a full range of sex-related toys and merchandise that you'd find in other sex shops – from cock rings to condoms and clitoral massagers to nipple clamps. But alongside the shelves of brightly colored designer vibrators, furry handcuffs, and hypoallergenic lubricants, what Azmi is really selling is a new idea about sex. A radiation therapist born and raised Indian Muslim in conservative Singapore, she's open about the personal journey the storefront represents. "I come from a culture where we don't acknowledge sex exists," Azmi notes. "I also work in healthcare, specifically in cancer. People were recovering from breast cancer or prostate cancer but no one was talking about sexual health post-recovery. I wanted to create an environment where we talk about the way sexual intimacy changes over the course of life. There's a lot of sensationalized sex in our culture, sex for the young and beautiful. But nobody talks about sex throughout life. Sex after kids, sex after menopause."

Come prepared to ask questions. Azmi and her staff will do there best to put you at ease. Offering programming that ranges from conversation groups for new moms and seniors to how-to seminars on Japanese rope bondage and introducing your partner to kink, Azmi's sex-positive approach nonetheless sees intimacy as the key. "How to do blowjobs is so yesterday," she quips. "Let's start with what's going on inside."

Address 557 5th Avenue, Brooklyn, NY 11215, +1 (718)780-6969, www.pleasenewyork.com | **Getting there** Subway to Prospect Avenue (R) | **Hours** Tue–Thu 2–9pm, Fri & Sat 2–10pm, Sun 2–7pm | **Tip** Hacienda Villa, a sex-positive intentional living community located in Williamsburg, also hosts regular educational and social events. Check out their website (www.wearehacienda.com) for more details.

84 Pratt Sculpture Park

A museum without walls in the heart of Fort Greene

Renowned for its premier schools of art and design, Pratt Institute is home to a world-class display of sculpture that few people know about, spread across the entirety of the 25-acre campus. Eclectic in form and style, this outdoor museum of three-dimensional art hosts more than 50 works at any given time, created in 1998 and curated until 2016 by David Weinrib, renowned sculptor and Pratt faculty member for some 30 years. *Public Art Review* recognized the park in 2006 as one of the 10 best college and university art collections nationally.

Describing his intent, Weinrib noted that choices were prompted less by concerns of style and renown than by the quality of the work. "I liken the Sculpture Park to a symphony," he wrote. "Our challenge is to bring all the parts in harmony." The analogy of orchestration is apt. Set within the green and open spaces while anchored by the campus' architectural gems, the pieces succeed individually but also resonate within the more complex landscape. Peer through Leon Smith's delicately poised steel-and-fiberglass minimalist creation, *Triangle* (2002), to frame Philip Grausman's monumental sculpted head, *Leucantha* (1988–93), whose smooth and rounded poly-resin face fixes its gaze firmly back at you. Or imagine yourself witnessing a primeval battle of skeletal kings of the jungle while standing before Wendy Klemperer's *Lions at the Gate* (2001). Everywhere you turn is a new visual experience until the boundary between natural and created becomes less fixed and certain, as in a work like David Henderson's *Skylark* (2005), where a propeller-like structure leans against a campus tree for its support.

While visiting the venerable institute, peer in on the Engine Room, located in the building with the tall smokestack. Installed in 1889, the steam engine still provides heat and hot water on campus.

Address 200 Willoughby Avenue, Brooklyn, NY 11205, +1 (718)636-3600, www.pratt.edu | Getting there Subway to Clinton Street–Washington Avenue (G) | Hours Unrestricted | Tip For other examples of public art, check out some of the borough's many murals. Red Hook boasts a work by the artist Swoon (at Pioneer Street and Conover Street), while the wall opposite the Stillwell Avenue station in Coney Island is the colorful canvas for the Brazilian "Os Gemeos," or "The Twins." Meanwhile, the work of Bushwick Collective artists takes center stage on walls near the intersection of Troutman Street at Saint Nicholas Avenue.

85 — Prison Ships Martyrs
A tomb for the Revolution's dead

High on the knoll that forms the center of Fort Greene Park sits a monument that most people pass regularly without pausing to learn its tragic history. Consisting of a stately, 149-foot-high Doric column made of Vermont granite and topped with a 7.5-ton bronze funerary urn forged at a foundry in Greenpoint, the monument pays homage to some 11,500 American patriots who perished during the American Revolution while jailed on the 16 British prison ships moored mostly along Brooklyn's shores in Wallabout Bay, roughly the site of the Brooklyn Navy Yard. Prisoners were crammed below decks in squalid conditions. One particularly appalling example is the HMS *Jersey*, a fully rigged British warship suited for 400 sailors that confined up to 1,100 American prisoners at a time. Abused and neglected by their captors, less than half of these prisoners survived. Far more soldiers died in captivity on these ships than were killed in the sum total of Revolutionary War battles.

Some of the dead are actually buried within a crypt beneath the monument. Originally tossed overboard into the East River or taken ashore and buried in shallow graves, body parts began to emerge from the makeshift cemetery with the ebb and flow of tidal erosion. Later, as the US Navy worked to expand the docks at the Navy Yard, enough bones to fill 20 large casks were uncovered during dredgings along the mucky shoreline and reburied nearby. By the 1870s, efforts were underway to find a more suitable memorial and resting place, especially after more remains were uncovered at the Navy Yard in 1899. Fort Greene Park, site of Fort Putnam in 1776, was chosen, with architect Stanford White overseeing much of the design of the monument.

President-elect William H. Taft was on hand for the dedication in November 1908. So when you go jogging in this lovely park, remember those who perished.

Address Washington Park Street, Brooklyn, NY 11205, +1 (718)722-3218, www.fortgreenepark.org, info@fortgreenepark.org | Getting there Subway to Dekalb Avenue (B, Q, R) or to Fulton Street (G) | Hours Daily 6–1am | Tip Visit the visitor's center near the monument for a display telling the history of the Battle of Brooklyn and of the British prison ships. Park Service Rangers are on hand to answer questions (www.nycgovparks.org/parks/fort-greene-park).

86 _ Raaka Virgin Chocolate

Your golden ticket inside the chocolate factory

"Bean-to-bar chocolate is different from most of what gets made," William Mullan, brand manager of this Red Hook specialty chocolate maker, clarifies from the start. "Most places essentially buy processed blocks, called *courvature,* that they melt down, resulting in a pretty homogenous quality." Instead, Raaka is part of a movement that began in the 90s, when chocolate makers began making their goods from scratch. "We wanted to bring a different flavor profile to people," Mullan says. "Cacao beans are actually fruit seeds. They have a really strong fruit-forward flavor, but when you roast them, much of that is lost. We saw unroasted chocolate as an opportunity to preserve these unique flavors." As a result, Raaka produces chocolates that taste brighter and bolder, flavors that, Mullan says, "make your mouth tingle."

Part of Raaka's fresh and unusual character comes from using single-bean infusions and developing recipes that release the distinctive qualities of each type of bean. For instance, one creation steams the fruity Peruvian cacao bean over simmering cabernet sauvignon wine, infusing the resulting chocolate with all of that flavor and aroma. Other varieties feature the flavors of ghost pepper, smoked chai, and cask-aged bourbon. These bars please sophisticated palettes, but anyone can fall in love with them.

Raaka buys beans directly from cooperatives of small-hold farmers in the Dominican Republic, Democratic Republic of Congo, Peru, and Tanzania, and from grower-centered organizations in those countries, paying a stable price above market rate. Mullan says, "The idea is to treat the growers we buy from as partners in the endeavor, and as value creators – not just suppliers."

Raaka offers tours and delicious tastings for a modest price on Saturday and Sunday afternoons, as well as chocolate-making classes.

Address 64 Seabring Street, Brooklyn, NY 11231, +1 (855)225-3354, www.raakachocolate.com, help@raakachocolate.com | **Getting there** Subway to Carroll Street (F, G) | **Hours** Mon–Fri 10am–5pm, Sat & Sun noon–6pm | **Tip** JoMart Chocolates has been feeding Brooklyn's sweet tooth since 1946. Try their famous chocolate dipped marshmallows or their mouthwatering caramel apples. Owner Michael Rogak, a third generation candy maker, offers private chocolate workshops (2917 Avenue R, Brooklyn, NY 11229, www.jomartchocolates.com).

87 Rainbow Bagel

This Williamsburg bakery sees the bagel as canvas

Not every bakery can say they created an internet sensation, but that's what happened in this bagel shop just steps from the L train in Williamsburg. Twice.

First, there was the bagel-croissant mash-up, the *cragel*. Blending that timeworn symbol of traditional Brooklyn, the bagel, with the emblem of European sophistication, the croissant, the cragel somehow manages to combine that substantial doughy *oomph* with the delicate flaky *aah*. Scot Rossillo, the owner and head baker of the Bagel Store who has been at this for more than two decades, makes two separate batters and delicately integrates them, somehow managing not to disturb the integrity of either, even retaining the central bagel hole. The only decision left is whether to wash it down with the conventional cup of joe or a cappuccino. A separate version folds in the sweetness of maple syrup and, well, bacon. That was 2013 – 14, when New York City was in the throes of "cronut-mania." While people in Manhattan lined up to score one of each day's limited edition pastries, Rossillo's dollars-and-cents Brooklyn approach meant that as the lines formed, he simply kept the oven on and made more cragels.

Just to prove he was no one-trick pony, Rossillo hit pay dirt again about two years later with his Rainbow Bagel. Bagel purists will no doubt do a double take at spying these rainbow-colored creations alongside the traditional bagels that fill the wire bins in Brooklyn bakery shelves from which your server plucks your choices. But though they might resist entertaining the idea of their venerable morning comfort food as a blank canvas, the flavor will win them over. They taste otherwise 100% traditional. Formed by creating layers of technicolored dough, Rossillo's tasty concoctions are served up with funfetti cream cheese topped with rainbow sprinkles. You might think you've hit a pot of gold – or a unicorn.

Address 754 Metropolitan Avenue, Brooklyn, NY 11211, +1 (718)782-5856,
www.thebagelstoreonline.com, thebagelstore@aol.com | Getting there Subway to Graham
Avenue (L) | Hours Daily 7am–6pm | Tip For a more traditional borough bagel experience,
try Shelsky's of Brooklyn in Boerum Hill (141 Court Street, Brooklyn, NY 112011,
www.shelskys.com). The deli offers a full selection of both cold- and hot-smoked fish, as well
as cream cheeses, salads, and spreads to top off your favorite bagel.

88 __ RBG's BKLYN

The beloved SCOTUS star's Brooklyn roots

Motown isn't the only home of Supremes. Fondly dubbed "Notorious RBG" by a New York University law student in an allusion to another famous Brooklynite, rapper Biggie Smalls, Ruth Bader Ginsburg is the rare Supreme Court judge to become a cultural icon. Transformed into a full-fledged internet meme following her rousing dissent in a 2013 voting rights case (when two digital media specialists took her image, added a crown inspired by Jean-Michel Basquiat, and the caption, "Can't spell truth without Ruth"), Justice Ginsburg is a paragon of achievement for champions of women's equality and the epitome of hope for liberal crusaders.

RBG's journey began right here in Brooklyn. Born to Russian-Jewish immigrants on March 15, 1933, Ginsburg grew up in a modest house in Midwood (1584 East 9th Street, Brooklyn, NY 11230). Born Joan Ruth Bader, her mother suggested she be called Ruth when there were a number of other Joans in her grade school class at PS 238 (633 East 8th Street, Brooklyn, NY 11218). Though the Baders were not devoutly religious, they did belong to the East Midwood Jewish Center (625 Ocean Avenue, Brooklyn, NY 11226), a Conservative synagogue where RBG studied Hebrew and learned about Judaism.

In her teens, RBG attended James Madison High School (3787 Bedford Avenue, Brooklyn, NY 11229), also attended by Senators Bernie Sanders and Chuck Schumer, as well as "Judge Judy" Sheindlin, singer Carole King, and comedian Chris Rock. Her senior yearbook lists her as cheerleader and baton twirler, and also as a cellist in the orchestra. An editor on the school paper, RBG contributed (in a nod to her future career) articles on the Magna Carta and the Bill of Rights.

Ginsburg went on to found the ACLU's Women's Rights project, arguing six cases before the Supreme Court (winning five), before her appointment to the high court by President Bill Clinton in 1993.

Address Various, see chapter | **Getting there** See mta.info for subway lines | **Hours** Unrestricted from the outside only | **Tip** Married to prominent international tax attorney Martin Ginsburg for 56 years until his death in 2010, RGB modeled gender equality in her personal life, too, where her husband famously did most of the cooking. His recipes (and family photos and momentos) were loving published as *Chef Supreme*, available to order at www.supremecourtgifts.org.

89__Red Hook Community Farm

Renewable farming and leaders sprout in Brooklyn

Created on the site of a former concrete baseball field in Red Hook, this pioneer urban farm yields more than 20,000 pounds of organically produced vegetables. Eggplant, peppers, tomatoes, beets, lettuces and three varieties of kale – these are just some of the harvest raised on this nearly three-acre plot.

Half the area is dedicated to a composting project, managed by staff from the Brooklyn Botanic Garden, which supplements the compost originally provided by the city's Department of Sanitation. The largest community composting site in the country run entirely by renewable resources, a handful of tumblers are placed near the Otsego Street entrance for the public to contribute household waste, like fruit and vegetable scraps and coffee grounds. Later, volunteers help process those contributions into usable, new, organic material (more than 200 tons annually) that gets added to the two-feet-deep raised beds where the food production takes place.

Farm operations are overseen by staff members from Added Value, an urban farming and food justice non-profit center, which has offices nearby. Focused on working with young people to cultivate knowledge about both sustainable farming and leadership skills, the group hires up to two dozen teen interns each year to work the farm after school and during the summer months. Public volunteers are always welcome, and there's no need to register in advance. Just come prepared for the weather and expect to get dirty. Regular drop-in opportunities offer a chance to work the garden or help with the compost.

Some produce from the garden is sold at the weekly farmers' market each Saturday morning. Subscriptions are also available that provide weekly distributions of the wide variety of fresh produce during the harvest season.

Address 560 Columbia Street, Brooklyn, NY 11231, +1 (718)288-6752, www.added-value.org | Getting there Subway to Smith Street–9 Street (F, G), then take bus B 57 or B 61 | Hours Fri 9am–noon, Sat 10:30am–1pm | Tip For another beautiful garden producing fruits and vegetables, drop in on the Bedford-Stuyvesant Community Garden (95 Malcolm X Boulevard, Brooklyn, NY 11221, www.nyrp.org).

90 Red Hook Swimming Pool
Summer relaxation in this FDR-era pool

1936 saw New York City, like most of the country, only just beginning to emerge from the throes of the Great Depression. A portion of that recovery came in the form of public works projects financed by FDR's Works Progress Administration. Under the direction of Mayor Fiorello LaGuardia and his controversial parks commissioner Robert Moses, the city won federal grants to create so many new swimming holes – eleven in all across all five boroughs – that the period from June through September that year was christened "the summer of pools." As well as providing a wellspring of much-needed jobs, the pools offered an equally desired opportunity for the long-suffering public living in underserved neighborhoods to relax and cool off as the temperatures soared. The kickoff for this Olympic-sized version in Red Hook, built to accommodate nearly 4,500 bathers, drew an enthusiastic crowd of 40,000.

Operating during the school summer holidays (late June to just after Labor Day), this pool is largely a family affair, with a few restrictions. Parks Department management advise against bringing floaties, electronics, or valuables. It's best to bring along a sturdy combination lock if you do need to bring personal items. Food and glass bottles are not permitted. Only white shirts and hats are permitted in the recreation area. Free sunscreen is available from dispensers on site.

Open daily, the pool closes from 3 to 4pm for cleaning. Serious swimmers can register online for early morning or night owl lap swimming. Check out the Parks website for details.

Also inaugurated in 1936, Williamsburg's even bigger McCarren Pool (776 Lorimer Street, Brooklyn, NY 11222) held 6,800 swimmers and still offers a chance to splish and splash. Meanwhile, the Sunset Park Pool (Seventh Avenue between 41st and 44th Streets), celebrated for its innovative underwater lighting at its opening, remains a hit.

Address 155 Bay Street, Brooklyn, NY 11231, +1 (718)772-3211, www.nycgovparks.org/
parks/red-hook-park | Getting there Subway to Carroll Street (F, G), then take bus B51 to
Lorraine Street–Henry Street | Hours Daily 11am–7pm with additional hours for lane
swimming | Tip Check out the Douglas and DeGraw Pool in Gowanus (250 Douglass
Street, Brooklyn, NY 11217, www.nycgovparks.org/parks/thomas-greene-playground) for
some smaller pool fun.

91 RetroFret Vintage Guitars

Love but with strings attached

A refuge for those with an affinity for acoustical craftsmanship, Retrofret Vintage Guitars is the beer drinker's equivalent of a craft brew for musicians. With antique and high-quality pieces curated by a knowledgeable and affable staff, the shop strives "to get things they like, not just what will sell."

The shop has its roots in owner Steve Uhrik's early interest in woodworking, which led him, as a teenager, to begin refurbishing and repairing vintage guitars. In the 1970s' and early 1980s' Uhrik owned a repair shop in SoHo, where occasionally (in that ancient pre-Craig's List era), he would help customers sell instruments, or he would buy pieces, mend them, then sell them on. Soon, he set up shop in Gowanus and established RetroFret.

Percussionists need not come here. RetroFret deals exclusively with stringed instruments, from cellos to mandolins, and banjos to ukuleles. Uhrik's staff include a team of luthiers, a fancy five-dollar word that describes those who construct and repair stringed instruments. (The word comes from the French word for lute.) But the RetroFret team is not only comprised of technicians. The group includes people who love guitars themselves – love their history and how they're made. Many among them, in fact, play, and the website bios include their choice of favorite guitars. Indeed, "play" is the perfect word: their joy in what they do is apparent.

With a showroom of over 300 pieces, some one-of-a-kind, you will be spoiled for choice. Whether you are looking to buy or just nerd out with like-minded music lovers, the shop is open and welcoming to the public and, more often than not, abuzz with the energy that's normally reserved for a hip gallery opening. In fact, that vibe is appropriate, since the shop's inventory is akin to an exhibition that comes complete with docents to provide context and help you better to see.

Address 87 Luquer Street, Brooklyn, NY 11231 +1 (718)237-4040, www.retrofret.com |
Getting there Subway to Carroll Street (F, G) or Smith–9th Street | Hours Mon–Fri
noon–7pm, Sat noon–6pm | Tip Brooklyn Lutherie (232 3rd Street, Suite E 003,
Brooklyn, NY 11215, www.brooklynlutherie.com) offers repair services from a pair of
professional musicians. Visits to their studio is by appointment only.

92 Roti at Ali's Trinidad

A local food vendor evokes memories of faraway

While the highlight for many in Brooklyn's vast West Indian community might be the annual New York City Caribbean Carnival Parade that occurs in late August, a multi-day bacchanal that draws several hundred thousand people annually to the streets where Crown Heights bumps up against Lefferts Garden, the rest of the year offers plenty of opportunities to celebrate their national heritage. A long history of immigration to the borough from the Caribbean islands has left Brooklyn blanketed in businesses, especially eateries, that provide reminders of home.

Ali's Trinidad Roti Shop does its part to supply a share of those gastronomic memories. Though the landscape is crowded with shops offering roti, an Indian-style flatbread that is used to wrap around potatoes and chickpeas along with your choice of meat, Ali's offerings stand out for their spicy blend of homey flavor. The shop is compact, and the service no-frills, but there's a reason people wait on line. And as you wait, you'll have time to strike up a conversation and, perhaps, listen to some calypso or soca.

Roti is actually a culinary legacy of the history of slavery and indentured servitude throughout the West Indies. For centuries the Caribbean was populated by enslaved African peoples forced to work on British-owned sugar cane plantations. Indentured South Asians arrived to take their place after abolition in the 1830s. They brought with them their delicious *naan* and *paratha* breads. It didn't take long for cultural crossover to occur.

Another Ali's Trinidad specialty is doubles (always said as a plural). Consisting of a pair of fried flat breads spiced with turmeric and filled with curried chickpeas like the Indian *chana*, the ones here are generously dressed with a sweet tamarind sauce or a pepper sauce. Wash it down with a ginger beer to complete the authentic island experience.

Address 1267 Fulton Street, Brooklyn, NY 11216, +1 (718)783-0316 | Getting there Subway to Franklin Avenue (C, S) | Hours Mon–Sat 11:30am–10pm | Tip To learn more about Caribbean food culture, or to explore other international culinary traditions, visit the Museum of Food and Drink (62 Bayard Street, Brooklyn, NY 11222, www.mofad.org).

93 Royal Palms Shuffleboard Club

Party like Grandma in the club

If sometimes life in Brooklyn feels like a college campus, Royal Palms sets the standard. Instead of the more standard bar with a pool table, the friendly competition of shuffleboard provides the framework for an evening out. Or is that "frenzied" competition? The game may seem relaxed and unhurried, the essence of suave, sophisticated cool. But sprinkle in a few of RPSC's signature cocktails or their seasonal offerings of craft beers from the stylish bar, with a sampling from one of the tasty food trucks on-site for the evening, and, before you know it, you won't have checked your text messages or email for an hour, and all that matters will be smack talking the opposition or the strategy and physics of a tiny disk.

Located on a hip stretch of Union Street in Gowanus, RPSC offers a spectacularly chill hang for a date night with other couples or makes for an inspired alternative to the after-work trip to the pub. The club is situated in a 17,000-square-foot warehouse decorated with enough palm trees and pink flamingos to leave you feeling you've been teleported to south Florida. That vibe is wholly intentional. The brainchild of Ashley Albert and Jonathan Schnapp, the inspiration came during a visit to Schnapp's grandmother, when a fun evening of shuffleboard brought back how vacations to Grandma's used to be.

A "cabana party" option means you'll have a booth to call home and a dedicated court. Otherwise, courts are first come, first served and come with a free five-minute lesson from a resident pro. While there may be waits, especially on league nights, to get your competitive juices flowing there are plenty of nostalgic games – Yahtzee!, Connect Four, and Jenga – to pass the time. A hip soundtrack, informed by an evening's particular food truck, makes the time pass quickly. A full schedule of the food trucks is available on RPSC's website.

Address 514 Union Street, Brooklyn, NY 11215, +1 (347)223-4410,
www.royalpalmsbrooklyn.com, info@royalpalmsshuffle.com | Getting there Subway to
Union Street (R) | Hours Mon–Thu 6pm–midnight, Fri 6pm–2am, Sat noon–2am,
Sun noon–10pm | Tip The Southern theme continues up the street at Pig Beach
(480 Union Street, Brooklyn, NY 11231, www.pigbeachnyc.com), which offers a delicious
array of barbecue treats. The outdoor beer garden is perfect for those warm summer
evenings with friends.

94 Salt Marsh Birdwatching
Gold medal nature center

When most people think of the 1936 Berlin Olympics, it's Jesse Owens who comes to mind. Only a few, however, know that the *first* American medal of those games came in the "Municipal Planning" portion of the "Arts" competitions: a silver medal for architect Charles Downing Lay for his redesign of the Marine Park neighborhood. It's true – from 1912 to 1948, athletics-inspired art and poetry were also Olympic competitions, probably inspired by the ancient Roman games. Emperor Nero added singing and poetry to the competition in 66 A.D. He won gold medals in both, no surprise to anyone.

Marine Park is home to the largest public park in Brooklyn, and more than half of its 798 acres consists of salt marshes like those that served as hunting and fishing grounds for the earliest Native American settlers. (Fire pits have been discovered that date from 800 to 1400 A.D.) Later, Dutch settlers also settled here, the marshland closely resembling the coastal plains of their homeland.

Though more than three-quarters of Jamaica Bay's large estuary wetland has disappeared (mostly due to development in the 1950s through 1970s), the remaining 18,000 acres play host to more than 325 species of birds and 50 species of butterflies, including many migratory birds passing through on their seasonal flights.

Formed in 2000, the Salt Marsh Nature Center is one of 10 Urban Park Ranger nature centers, making it ideal as a weekend activity spot for families. Pack a camera, binoculars, and a water bottle, and head out onto one of the well-groomed trails, offering a chance to experience the fragile ecosystem close up. Ramble through the grasslands alongside briny Gerritsen Creek. Well-placed benches provide perfect viewing spots to observe the herons, cormorants, egrets, ducks, and geese as they make their way among the shallow waters, as redwinged blackbirds and marsh hawks soar overhead.

Address 3302 Avenue U, Brooklyn, NY 11234, +1 (718)421-2021, www.saltmarshalliance.org |
Getting there Subway to Avenue U (Q), bus B 3 to Avenue U / East 33rd Street | Hours
Grounds and trails open daily dawn – dusk; Salt Marsh Nature Center: Sat & Sun noon – 4pm
in summer | Tip Across the street in Marine Park, Wheel Fun Rentals (9000 Bay Parkway,
Brooklyn, NY 11229, www.wheelfunrentals.com) rents bicycles, tandems, and surreys by the
hour, as well as kayaks and paddleboards.

95__San Germán Records

Spirit and sounds of the island

Radamés Millán has seen the neighborhood change. Though he doesn't look it, he's in his mid-70s, but he started San Germán Records when he was only 17. Then, the community was almost all transplanted islanders, so much so that the south end of nearby Graham Avenue was known as "Avenue of Puerto Rico." Now, with East Williamsburg gentrifying, his shop is an island toehold in the middle of a largely young, prosperous, white community. That change makes a difference, mostly in how the shop is experienced on the street. "In the old days, I would have had the music playing loud – salsa, bolero, merengue. Now, if you play the music too loud, people will call the police."

Named for a region in southwest Puerto Rico, San Germán Records is an homage to Millán's homeland. Not just a record store, this is the one-stop shop for all things Puerto Rican. Whether it's a coffee mug, ball cap, keychain, or license plate frame, Millán offers a wide selection of flag-adorned tchotchkes. Flags also emblazon T-shirts, curtains, bed sheets, and onesies for that special newborn. Roberto Clementé is seen here too, among the Puerto Rican pantheon, as are J-Lo, Ricky Martin, and Rita Moreno. Shelves full of bongos, congas, *claves* and *güiros* will give you everything you need to play along with the salsa cassettes and CDs displayed on tables out on the street.

A ready conversationalist, Millán takes his role as cultural ambassador to the community seriously as well. For the past two decades, he's organized the community's Three Kings Parade, keeping alive these cultural traditions even in the face of a community transformation.

Check out Johnny Albino Music Center, across the street at 88 Moore Street, for another chance to experience the charm of the old neighborhood. Founded by and named for the famed bolero singer who recorded more than 300 albums, the focus is on musical instruments.

Address 89 Moore Street, Brooklyn, NY 11206, +1 (718)218-7355, www.sangermanrecords.com, tiendasangerman@gmail.com | **Getting there** Subway to Flushing Avenue (J, M) | **Hours** Mon–Thu 10am–7pm, Fri & Sat 10am–7:30pm, Sun 11am–5pm | **Tip** The Little Caribbean Cultural District, celebrating immigrants from throughout the West Indies, was designated in 2017 and encompasses the area within the triangle defined by Flatbush, Nostrand, and Church Avenues. See website for details about food crawls, art walks, and much more (www.littlecaribbean.nyc).

96___Secret Tomato Sauce at L&B Spumoni Gardens

A sauce you can't refuse

In Bensonhurst, they take their pizza very seriously. So seriously, in fact, that when a former employee of this longtime local favorite opened a pizzeria in Staten Island with conspicuously similar tasting sauce, the mob got involved. According to later testimony, members from the Colombo crime family (one of whom just happened to be an in-law of the offended L&B owners) paid the rival pizzeria a visit, threatening the owner and demanding a payoff of $75,000. Ultimately, $4,000 changed hands to settle the offense.

L&B (as it's known by regulars) opened 80 years ago when immigrant Ludavico Barbati learned how to make pizza in the garage of a local baker. Using a cart drawn by Babe the horse, Barbati sold first pizza, then later spumoni (a tasty low-fat form of ice cream named for the Italian word meaning "sea foam" because of its light, airy quality) throughout Bensonhurst and Gravesend. As demand increased, Barbati bought the lot where the business still stands and, with the help of friends and tradesmen from the Old Country, built a small structure to house his production. Over time, people would come to the factory to buy his pizza and spumoni until, by the 1950s, the pizzeria was added.

Now in its fourth generation of Barbati family ownership, L&B-still offers its signature zesty blend of herbs on both Sicilian and thin-crust round pies. Prepared "upside down" style – with the sauce on top of the mozzarella cheese – each bite offers a spicy explosion of flavor.

The dining room menu offers Italian favorites from carbonara and calamari to ziti and zuppa di pesce. Pizza by the slice (strictly no toppings) is available at the walk-up window and can be enjoyed as you people-watch outside. Don't forget to save room for the dessert!

Address 2725 86th Street, Brooklyn, NY 11223, +1 (718)449-1230, www.spumonigardens.com | Getting there Subway to 25 Avenue U (F), to 86 Street (D) | Hours See website for seasonal hours | Tip Pizza lovers should also pay a visit to Totonno's Pizzeria Napolitano in the heart of Coney Island (1524 Neptune Avenue, Brooklyn, NY 11224). Serving pies since 1924, Totonno's is the oldest continually-run family-owned pizzeria in America!

97 __ The Sketchbook Project

An art project that draws the world

Steven Peterman, founder of The Brooklyn Art Library's Sketchbook Project, never much cared for the gallery system. He didn't think his work was good enough to hang on a gallery wall, but he wanted to create art anyway. It was 2006, and pay-to-participate art projects were beginning to pop up on the internet. "We wanted to do the opposite," Peterman says. "This was about a year or so before crowdsourcing, so we really didn't know what to call it, but we knew if everyone gets together this really cool art project could happen."

Peterman and his collaborators quickly realized that sketchbooks could be a unique way for people to share their stories in a less pressured way. "When people are doing paintings that hang on the wall, they are intimidated about what they want to share," he observed. "With sketchbooks, people have this sense that they can hide it away. We found that people were sharing amazing ideas." Almost as importantly, sketchbooks provided an easy – and standard – format for people all over the world to contribute.

Forty thousand sketchbooks later, the "really cool art project" is an archive of work from artists of all ages and over 135 countries. Housed in a bright, stylish space in Williamsburg since 2009, its back table is a great place to spend some time poring through that day's selection of books. "They run the gamut," Peterman says, "from professional artists who use it as the chance to be free, to first-time artists who are afraid of the process but trying to get out of their comfort zone." He notes that a portion even use their sketchbook as a way of dealing with some kind of hardship in their life.

A small shop offers the standard 5" x 7" sketchbook that must be used for all submissions, after which the book will be barcoded and shelved in the collection. For an additional fee, books are digitized and live online as well and are tagged by artist, location, medium, and theme.

Address 28 Frost Street, Brooklyn, NY 11211, +1 (718)388-7941, www.thesketchbookproject.com, hello@sketchbookproject.com | Getting there Subway to Metropolitan Avenue (G), or to Lorimer Street (L) | Hours Wed–Sun 10am–6pm | Tip Hone your own skills by attending a Friday Night Drink and Draw Meetup session, offered regularly in Greenpoint. Each three-hour session is available for a small fee and offers an opportunity to work from a live model (www.meetup.com/greenpointfiguredrawing). Locations vary.

98__ Sportsmen's Row
The sport of Kings – County, that is

"We forget how significant horse racing was as a spectator sport," Lucas Rubin observes as he sets the background for understanding the unique history of an area of Park Slope's 8th Avenue between St. Johns and Lincoln Places. Author of the book *Sportsmen's Row*, Rubin reminds that the moniker derived from the fact that, for a time, a single block played home to Philip and Michael Dwyer, a pair of stable-owning brothers, and two of horse racing's finest jockeys. "Far and away the first large-scale spectator sport was horse racing. It was the first sport to charge entrance fees to watch a competition, was heavily connected with the development of mass media and, of course, was central to the development of gambling. High status individuals like August Belmont simultaneously bumped up against some of the outer fringes of society. There's an interesting mix of wealth and poverty, wealth and criminality. What's lost is that we just don't see horses anywhere in our regular lives. When the horse drove everything, it was natural to be interested in displays of strength and speed."

The Dwyers were butchers, but in the early 1870s, they began assembling a stable of elite thoroughbreds. Winning the Kentucky Derby twice, the Preakness once, and the Belmont Stakes five times between 1883 and 1888, the brothers used part of their winnings to finance beautiful homes close to Prospect Park. Philip owned adjoining Romanesque Revival five-story brownstones at no. 8–10, while Michael lived in no. 26. The Dwyers' premier jockeys – Jim McLaughlin, winner of a record six Belmonts (no. 24), and Edward "Snapper" Garrison, with more than 700 career wins (no. 30) – finished off the cluster.

The Montauk Club (no. 25), the last of the great Victorian social clubs, was modeled after the Ca'd'Oro in Venice. Completed in 1891, it contains beautiful terracotta friezes depicting scenes of the Montauk tribe.

Address 8th Avenue between St. Johns Place and Lincoln Place, Brooklyn, NY 11217 | Getting there Subway to Grand Army Plaza (2, 3), or to 7 Avenue (B, Q) | Hours Unrestricted from the outside only | Tip Be sure to visit the Grand Army Plaza Greenmarket Saturdays 8am–4pm (Prospect Park West and Flatbush Avenue, Brooklyn, NY 11238, www.grownyc.org/greenmarket/brooklyn-grand-army-plaza). Celebrating its 30th year in 2018, it is the flagship market in Brooklyn.

99__ St. Mary's Star of the Sea
Where wedding bells rang for the Capones

While most everyone knows of the gangster's Chicago mob connections, not everyone is aware of Al Capone's Brooklyn roots. One of nine children, Alphonse Gabriel Capone was born in 1899 to Italian immigrant parents in the top-floor apartment at 95 Navy Street, where the family moved soon after their arrival in 1895 from Salerno. A baker by trade, like many immigrants, Capone's father Gabriele reinvented himself as a barber in America, while his mother Teresa worked as a seamstress. At three weeks old, Capone was baptized at St. Mary the Archangel Church (which was located at the intersection of Tillary and Lawrence Streets), the center of the downtown neighborhood's Italian Catholic community.

When Al was eight, the Capones moved to 38 Garfield Street, living above Gabriele's new barbershop in the more ethnically mixed bottom end of Park Slope, his father a newly minted citizen. Capone's biographer Deidre Bair has written that the gangster grew up squarely thinking of himself as American not Italian, and would correct anyone who made the mistake of suggesting otherwise.

Capone came under the spell of mobster Johnny Torrio in his early teens, becoming a bagman at bars and brothels, a job that led Capone to his underworld life and also directly to the syphilis and gonorrhea that ravaged him later and led to his early death at age 48.

Capone met Mae Josephine Coughlin in late 1917, when she was an office worker in the bottle factory where he also worked. Irish and two years Al's senior, Mae quickly became pregnant. Her disapproving mother refused to allow a quick marriage. Beir suggests that Mae's mother may have secretly hoped that a difficult pregnancy might end in a miscarriage and eliminate the need to wed. In fact, the child Sonny was two months premature in December 1918. The couple wed three weeks later at the charming 1851 church, St. Mary's Star of the Sea.

Address 467 Court Street, Brooklyn, NY 11231, +1 (718)625-2270, www.stmarystarbrooklyn.com | Getting there Subway to Carroll Street (F, G) | Hours See website for daily mass schedule | Tip While Capone served as a bartender at the Harvard Inn in Coney Island (formerly located on the Bowery at Seaside Walk) for Torrio protégé Frankie Yale, gangster Frank Galluccio took offense at Capone's repeated insults to his kid sister. Capone received the wound that earned him the nickname "Scarface."

100__Sunny's Bar

You want to go where nobody knows your name

Consider this a twist on that famous TV bar: unless you're a regular, this is a place you wanna go where nobody will know your name (though they'll all know each others'). Perch yourself on one of the wobbly stools next to the bar of this old Red Hook watering hole that comes complete with Duane Eddy or Gram Parsons' records on the turntable, creaky uneven floorboards, and several strands of colored lights that look like they came off a Christmas tree 40 years ago. Order up a $3 can of Narragansett and just take it all in.

There's only a small sign that says "BAR" along cobblestoned Conover Street to let you know you've arrived. A throwback to the Red Hook of old, dominated by hardworking dockworkers, fishermen, with a few shady scoundrels on the side, Sunny's is what one chronicler labeled "the neighborhood's spiritual outpost," filled with creatures of habit looking for nirvana in bar form every night of the week.

For years, the place was operated by Sunny Balzano, the garrulous fourth-generation family proprietor of a place with roots to the 1890s, who was such a reluctant saloon-keeper that for years the place was only opened one night a week and ran largely on the honor system without a liquor license. Eventually all that informality went the way of the dinosaurs, but what remained was quite enough. After Balzano passed away in 2016, patrons helped his widow raise enough money to buy out the band of relatives inclined to sell. It was important to keep the place in the family, in other words, even if not a family defined by blood. Just a few years prior, that same band of regulars rescued the place after Hurricane Sandy's ravages.

Regular bluegrass/folk and country jams happen Saturday nights at 9pm in the room at the back. A few tables offer a chance to sit outside, while the front sidewalk offers near-perfect views of the sunset. Nirvana indeed.

Address 253 Conover Street, Brooklyn, NY 11231, +1 (718)625-8211,
www.sunnysredhook.com, info.sunnysbar@gmail.com | Getting there Subway to Jay
Street–Metrotech (A, N), to Dekalb Avenue (Q), or to Borough Hall (2, 3), then bus
B 61 to Beard Street–Van Brunt Street | Hours Mon 5pm–midnight, Tue 4pm–2am,
Wed–Fri 4pm–4am, Sat 11–4am, Sun 11am–midnight | Tip If the night is right, take
the five-minute walk down to the pier at Louis Valentino, Jr. Park (Ferris Street and Coffey
Street, Brooklyn, NY 11231, www.nycgovparks.org/parks/valentino-pier/history). Named
for a Brooklyn firefighter who lost his life returning to a blaze in search of wounded
colleagues, the spot offers a gorgeous expansive view of Lady Liberty and the harbor.

101__Sunshine Laundromat

Finally, a place to use up those extra quarters

Metropolitan Avenue in Greenpoint may very well play host to the business that epitomizes Brooklyn hipster cool. From street level, this laundromat looks, well, like a laundromat – rows of stainless-steel double- and triple-loading washers on one side, and a wall of oversized drying machines on the other. A couple of old-school pinball machines sitting up front in the window add a bit of a hint, but ultimately give very little away. Walk straight through the aisle and open what looks like another dryer in the back, however, and you will find yourself time-warped into a vintage 1980s' pinball arcade paradise.

The brainchild of owner Peter Rose, the backroom features about two dozen machines from this golden era of pinball, including Jurassic Park, Houdini, Indiana Jones, Star Trek and Addams Family. Most of these classic games are still offered at the period-appropriate price of three balls for 75¢. A bar featuring mosaic tables Rose designed with his mother that show his dogs drinking, eating, and playing pinball, offers eight varieties on tap. The bathrooms even pay homage to pinball courtesy of a flush handle designed like a pinball flipper and lights that, with a few too many, could leave you feeling you've stepped inside a game. A wide selection of board games, from Connect Four to Trouble, offers alternative laundry-waiting strategies for non-pinballers. Late hours mean you can even squeeze a drink, fun, *and* a load of laundry into the wee hours of the night.

If Asteroids, Donkey Kong, or Pac-Man are more your thing, grab a Lyft over to Barcade at 388 Union Avenue. Founded in 2004 and now franchised in several cities, the original started in a warehouse here in Williamsburg. With a selection of around 50 early electronic game consoles that include Tetris, Galaga, Centipede, and Frogger, you'll have a range of choices on even the busiest night.

Address 860 Manhattan Avenue, Brooklyn, NY 11222, +1 (718)475-2055, www.sunshinelaundromat.com, info@barcadebrooklyn.com | **Getting there** Subway to Greenpoint Avenue (G) | **Hours** Bar: Mon–Thu 4pm–2am, Fri & Sat 4pm–4am, Sun noon–2am; Laundromat: Mon–Thu 7–2am, Fri & Sat 7–4am, Sun 8–2am | **Tip** Prefer bowling? Try The Gutter (200 North 14th Street, Brooklyn, NY 11249, www.thegutterbrooklyn.com) in Williamsburg. With eight lanes and a bar, haul out that vintage bowling league shirt you invested in and put it to actual use!

102 Torah Animal World

A menagerie worthy of Noah

Visitors to Torah Animal World, a project of the Living Torah Museum in a two-story Borough Park row house, are in for a unique treat. Named the "hands-down, no-contest" no. 1 on the *Village Voice's* list of Strangest Museums of NYC in 2015, the collection came about from the singular vision of Rabbi Shaul Shimon Deutsch to gather all the animals appearing in the Torah. Deciding a museum was more practical than a zoo, Rabbi Deutsch turned undeterred to the community of taxidermists and circulated a list of what he was after.

Now, 10 years and 500 animals later, three rooms are chock-a-block full of beasts of every kind. Full bodied examples of a lioness, ostrich, and camel sit alongside wall mounts of an African elephant, rhinoceros, and a bison. Rabbi Deutsch encourages a hands-on approach for young visitors, believing "if you touch history, history touches you." He adds that this sometimes means making adjustments. "We had to file down the teeth of that crocodile so no one would get hurt," Rabbi Deutsch says, perching himself on a stool made from an elephant's leg. "Where else can kids experience how hairy an elephant's skin is?" He also points out a few of the more exotic elements of the collection – for example, a 600-year-old egg from an elephant bird, a now-extinct flightless bird of Madagascar, and the musk deer, now native to Siberia but during biblical times found in Mesopotamia and characterized by a pair of saber-like fangs. A separate gallery of the museum includes animals mentioned in the rabbinical writings of the Talmud, including many unusual birds of prey.

While the original focus was Bible study, the audience has grown wider over time. Forty percent of visitors are now non-Jewish, many coming to see the rarities of his collection, others to sketch the animals or to study animal anatomy. In all, more than 1.3 million have made the trek.

Address 1603 41st Street, Brooklyn, NY 11218, +1 (877)752-6286, www.torahanimalworld.com | Getting there Subway to Ditmas Avenue (F) | Hours Sun–Thu 9am–9pm, Fri 9am–2pm by appointment only | Tip The Living Torah Museum houses artifacts donated by Dr. Donald Moore, last remaining survivor of the excavation of King Tut's tomb. Tours are available in Hebrew, Yiddish, or English, for children or adults.

103 — Triangle Shirtwaist Factory Fire Memorial

Remembering a tragic moment in labor history

As the final resting place for more than half a million of Brooklyn's dead, Cemetery of the Evergreens offers many stories to tell. Bill "Bojangles" Robinson, the great African-American dancer and actor, is here, as is Sante Righini, *Titanic* victim. Pioneer animator Winsor McCay, whose work was unrivaled until Walt Disney, is among the interred. So is pianist Blind Tom Wilkins, born a slave and now considered an autistic savant, who became the first African-American performer to give a command White House performance when he played for President Buchanan in 1860.

One memorial of particular note in the cemetery commemorates six victims of the 1911 Triangle Shirtwaist Factory Fire. The deadliest industrial accident in New York City's history, the fire claimed 146 lives and caused outrage as the horrific details and circumstances of those deaths emerged. The factory, a blouse-making operation that employed mainly immigrant women working 52-hour weeks at low wages, caught fire. The factory was situated on the eighth, ninth, and tenth floors of the building (still standing at 23–29 Washington Place in Greenwich Village), and later investigations investigations revealed doors to stairwells and exits were routinely locked to prevent theft. As a result, more than 50 leaped to their death. The incident spurred important improvements in working conditions, especially for garment workers.

So badly burned that they could not be identified, six victims were interred together here beneath a stone monument depicting a kneeling woman, head bowed in grief. Thousands lined the streets for their procession. It was only in 2011, at the 100th anniversary of the fire, that amateur historian Michael Hirsch solved the mystery, leaving the five women and one man nameless no more.

IN SYMPATHY AND SORROW
CITIZENS OF NEW YORK
RAISE THIS MONUMENT
OVER THE GRAVES OF
UNIDENTIFIED WOMEN AND
CHILDREN WHO WITH ONE
HUNDRED AND THIRTY NINE
OTHERS PERISHED BY FIRE IN
THE TRIANGLE SHIRTWAIST
FACTORY WASHINGTON PLACE
MARCH 25 1911

Address 1626 Bushwick Avenue, Brooklyn, NY 11207, +1 (718)455-5300, www.theevergreenscemetery.com, info@theevergreenscemetery.org | **Getting there** Subway to Broadway Junction (A, C, J, L, M, Z) | **Hours** Daily 8am–4:30pm | **Tip** Nearby Cypress Hills Cemetery, which also straddles the boundary of Brooklyn and Queens, contains the graves of notables such as baseball star and civil rights pioneer Jackie Robinson, artist Piet Mondrian, and Brooklyn-native sex symbol Mae West (833 Jamaica Avenue, Brooklyn, NY 11208, www.cypresshillscemetery.org).

IN MEMORY OF
JOSEPHINE CAMMARATA
DORA EVANS
MAX FLORIN
MARIA GIUSEPPA LAULETTI
CONCETTA PRESTIFILIPPO
FANNIE ROSEN

104__ Van Brunt Stillhouse

A farm distillery in the big city

It would be a difficult decision for anyone to walk away from steady work on a highly successful television show for the risky role of a new business owner. But that's just what Daric Schlesselman did back in 2011 when he left his job as editor of *The Daily Show* to co-found Van Brunt Stillhouse with his wife, Sarah Ludington. "I was more of a consumer of spirits that a maker of spirits. I made beer and cider at home," Schlesselman remembers. "And then one New Year's I decided to buy a still and make some brandy at home. I was doing a lot of fruit picking and wanted to plant some fruit trees and explore the possibility of trying something new."

That something was a whiskey distillery, named for Cornelius Van Brunt, one of the Dutch colonial Breukelen's founding fathers who farmed the Gowanus canal area. Schlesselman needed to look no farther than Red Hook, already his home for several years and, he affirms passionately, "hands down the most neighborhood-y place I ever lived." That sense of community was vital when Hurricane Sandy arrived. "We immediately came together. It was very natural, something we already did."

That same sense of care is present in Schlesselman's tasty libations. Ingredients are sourced from small growers in upstate New York, allowing Van Brunt to be classified a "farm distillery" despite its urban setting. As master distiller, he creates every recipe, crafted with a chemist's sense of experimentation and precision plus an artist's sense of knowing when the canvas is just right. The processes are as old as Roman invasions of Scotland, but the product is uniquely his, the smooth American Whiskey with a wonderful blend of grains, or the VBS single malt, aged for nine months in small, new oaken casks.

Tours of the distillery are available several times weekly and include a $10 voucher off any bottle purchased.

Address 6 Bay Street, 1st floor, Brooklyn, NY 11231, +1 (718)852-6405, www.vanbruntstillhouse.com, info@vanbruntstillhouse.com | **Getting there** Subway to Jay Street–Metrotech (A, C) and bus B 57 to Dwight Street–Dikeman Street, or subway to Smith–9th Street (F, G) and bus B 61 to Lorraine Street–Oswego Street | **Hours** Thu–Fri 4–9pm, Sat 2–9pm, Sun 2–8pm | **Tip** Book a tour or stop by the tasting room at King's County Distillery. Founded in 2010, it is the borough's oldest modern whiskey distillery, and the first to open since Prohibition (299 Sands Street, Building 121, Brooklyn, NY 11205, www.kingscountydistillery.com).

105 Victorians in Ditmas Park

You're walking in a dreamscape, but it's all real

As you wander through this hidden pocket of Brooklyn, you will be transported back to the 19th century. Though Brooklyn brownstones have become the symbol that comes to mind when conjuring the borough, a patch of neighborhood just south of Prospect Park hosts more than 2,000 Victorian-era houses in styles that include Tudor, Queen Anne, Colonial Revival, and Georgian. These beautiful, single-family homes seem hopelessly out of place. Wood-framed with wraparound front porches and gabled roofs, Victorian gems are spread over a small area just minutes from the bustle of Flatbush Avenue. With many houses protected by the Landmarks Preservation Commission, this enclave retains its unique character in spite of the rapid refashioning of other tracts of Brooklyn real estate.

The best way for exploring here is to put shoe leather to pavement. Step onto the Q train, exiting at Church Avenue, and head south to the west of the rail line. If you think you've somehow wandered onto a movie set, it's because you have. Pay a visit to the gorgeous house at 101 Rugby Road, completed in 1903 for Civil War Colonel Alexander Bacon, later a successful lawyer. In 1982, then painted pink, the exterior served as the boarding house run by Holocaust survivor Meryl Streep in *Sophie's Choice*. Across the street, at no. 100, is a home built to resemble a Swiss chalet, positioned next to one in the Spanish Mission style.

Another home with a film connection can be found at 1320 Ditmas Avenue, a neo-Tudor occupying a corner lot, rumored to have been occupied by Hollywood legends Mary Pickford and Douglas Fairbanks during their days working for American Vitagraph, a prominent silent film studio that operated nearby.

Finally, don't miss the houses on Buckingham Road between Caton and Albemarle Roads, none more compelling than no. 131, which incorporates Asian elements in the design.

Address The area between Church Avenue and Newkirk Avenue, and between Flatbush Avenue and Ocean Avenue | Getting there Subway to Church Avenue (Q) | Hours Unrestricted from the outside only | Tip The nearby Prospect Park Parade Grounds is a lively area with multiple sports facilities. According to NYCGo, "more than 40 World Series rings have been awarded to players who started their careers playing here, including Sandy Koufax and Manny Ramirez." (Coney Island Avenue, Brooklyn, NY 11218, www.nycgo.com/venues/prospect-park-parade-ground)

106___ View from Fairway Market

Enjoy a cup of joe with Lady Liberty and the gulls

Even on a stormy evening – maybe *especially* on a stormy evening – locals know that the little outdoor café behind the Fairway Market is the perfect place to be. While beautiful sunset-daubed skies stretching across the horizon will probably always be the preferred Instagram post, especially when they frame a seafoam-tinged Statue of Liberty that looks close enough to touch, there's a certain sublime magnificence to watching the heavens darken and become blanketed by gray.

Walk through the store to the back, grab a coffee or a sandwich from the café counters, then pull up one of the chairs outside. To the West and New Jersey, working elements of the harbor are on full display. Cranes load and offload colossal container ships that circumnavigate the globe, as a fleet of tugs and ferries plug away doing their daily grind. In front of you, lights twinkle along the shoreline of Staten Island as barges to and fro through the strait and beneath the graceful Verrazano arch. Listen carefully, and you'll hear the clamoring of clanging bells from navigational buoys bobbing in the same choppy water that laps against the boulders forming the protective embankments.

In late October 2012, this was ground zero for Hurricane Sandy. Dubbed "Frankenstorm" by the media, Red Hook residents endured waist-high flooding of area streets, loss of electricity that lingered for weeks, and property loss that was among the worst in the city. Because the area is not only low in profile but also only two to three meters above the water table – Red Hook originally was swampy marshland when the Dutch arrived in 1636 – flooding came from below as well as from the harbor. Housed in the ground floor of an 1860s'-era warehouse, one of several nearby, Fairway had to be completely gutted. Miraculously, the gourmet grocery was able to re-open a mere four months after Sandy, well ahead of schedule.

Address 480-500 Van Brunt Street, Brooklyn, NY 11231, +1 (718)254-0923, www.fairwaymarket.com | Getting there Subway to Jay Street–MetroTech (F) or Dekalb Avenue (Q, R), then bus B 61 to Beard Street–Van Brunt Street | Hours Daily 7am–10pm | Tip For another Red Hook treat, take a 10-minute stroll over to Steve's Authentic Key Lime Pie (185 Van Dyke Street, Brooklyn, NY 11231, www.keylime.com), where pies are mouthwatering and the lime juice is always 100% fresh squeezed.

107 War Heroes' Mass Grave

The sacrifice of the First Maryland Regiment

A rusting plaque on a Legion hall and a graffiti-covered mural next to a parking lot are about all that mark the mass grave of the American Revolutionary War's earliest heroes. Facing off a mere eight weeks after the Declaration of Independence was issued by the Continental Congress, maneuvering began with British troops landing on Staten Island, and then advancing on Brooklyn. On August 22, 1776, General William Howe transported 15,000 troops to Gravesend Bay, where they were joined by 5,000 Hessians. With astute scouting, the British moved 4,000 troops across the Gowanus Canal toward the American position in Brooklyn Heights, where there were 10,000 troops. Meanwhile, the main body of Howe's army (10,000 troops under General Clinton) were sent to flank the Americans and catch them unaware.

At 2am on August 27th, the Battle of Brooklyn began when American troops fired shots on Redcoats advancing near the Red Lion Inn (now Green-Wood Cemetery). General George Washington had moved 1,500 troops to cover the pass toward Brooklyn Heights, but they were quickly overwhelmed by British soldiers led by General Cornwallis, who pushed on to the Vechte-Cortelyou farmhouse (see ch. 20). The First Maryland Regiment, also known as the "Maryland 400," commanded by American General William Alexander (Lord Stirling), were left to divert the enemy so that the remaining Patriot troops could fall back. Six times they charged the British line, only to be repelled and sustain heavy losses. When finally ordered to join the retreat, the remaining soldiers became mired in the marshy Gowanus Creek, sitting targets to British musket fire. Less than a dozen of the roughy 270 men of this squad survived. "They fought like wolves," Cornwallis later said. Observing from his position, General Washington lamented, "Good God, what brave men I must this day lose."

Address 193 9th Street, Brooklyn, NY 11215 | Getting there Subway to
4 Avenue–9 Street (F, G, R) | Hours Unrestricted from the outside only | Tip
A memorial commemorating the Maryland 400, engraved with General Washington's
quote, is located on Lookout Hill in Prospect Park. Enter the park at the Vanderbilt
Street Playground from Prospect Park Southwest and follow Wellhouse Drive to the
left (www.nycgovparks.org/parks/prospect-park/highlights/19641).

108__ Watertower

A Brooklyn icon transformed and illuminated

"I'm kind of a rooftop guy," artist Tom Fruin says casually. He's poised on a subsection of the DUMBO building where his studio is located. Behind him, three wooden water towers, like the ones seen atop buildings all over Brooklyn, form part of the neighborhood cityscape. In front of him, his gorgeous sculpted *Watertower* (this first one was created in 2012) sits perched against the backdrop of the Manhattan Bridge.

Fruin moved to New York from LA in the late 90s, and the water towers were one of the first things to catch his eye. "They're a very organic shape. Not only is it filled with water, but it's round and made from a natural material – wood – and they're kind of perched like sentinels on almost every building, especially in this industrial neighborhood. It seemed like an overlooked but iconic shape, an infrastructural element that was everywhere but that you took for granted. And I thought if I could transform one, to make it somewhat fantastical, it would force the viewer to reconsider their surroundings and appreciate everything else that is going on."

The artist began by measuring wooden tanks, then designing his own to fit in with the others. (It is 10 feet high and 10 feet in diameter, with a 3-foot-high working roof.) Fruin used found and salvaged materials – plexiglass scraps from local sign shops or from the studios of friends. "It's like a quilt," Fruin observes. "The scraps aren't useful to a sign shop. But I can add little teeny bits of things together and make something larger." About 1,000 scraps went into this work. "I also like that sign shop materials are inherently the colors of this community."

Each night, Fruin's *Watertower* also puts on a show. Using the open source program Arduino, a computer-savvy friend created an hour-long lighting sequence for the seven lights tucked inside that repeats from dusk to dawn.

Address 20 Jay Street, Brooklyn, NY 11201, www.tomfruin.com/watertower.html, tom@tomfruin.com | Getting there Subway to York Street (F) | Hours Unrestricted from the outside only | Tip Other Watertower sculptures may be viewed at Brooklyn Heights (Grace Court, Brooklyn, NY 11201), and atop Greenpoint Beer and Ale Co. (7 North 15th Street, Brooklyn, NY 11222).

109 Weeksville Heritage Center

Pathway from freedom to citizenship

Hidden in plain site in what is now Crown Heights, Weeksville Heritage Center celebrates one of America's first free African-American communities, whose history came close to being lost. Only the timely intervention in 1968 of Pratt professor James Hurley and a community-led campaign saved four Hunterfly Road properties that today serve as exhibition spaces to tell the story.

Named for James Weeks, a dockworker and ex-slave who purchased two lots here in 1838, little more than a decade after slavery ended in New York, Weeksville played an important role in securing the African-American vote. Though white men could vote without restriction, Black men were required to hold $250 in property, a condition met by only a dozen Black New Yorkers. Home ownership here became an important means of propelling free African-Americans into the ranks of full citizenship.

Though a part of Brooklyn, Weeksville operated initially as an independent African-American enclave, serving as a center of Black activism and a safe haven, especially after the passage of the Fugitive Slave Act. Journalist Junius Morel, who wrote for the abolitionist newspaper *The North Star*, lived here, as did Rufus Perry, an escaped slave who became a minister and educator. Both men also served in the African Civilization Society, the foremost Black rights organization at the center of conversations about colonizing Liberia as a free Black state.

Weeksville also nurtured strong women leaders. Dr. Susan Smith McKinney, New York's first African-American doctor, lived here, co-founding a hospital and operating an integrated practice. Sarah Garnet, her sister, became the first African-American public school principal at a local grammar school in 1863.

A guided tour will alllow you to peek inside the Hunterfly houses.

Address 158 Buffalo Avenue, Brooklyn, NY 11213, +1 (718)756-5250 ext. 300, www.weeksvillesociety.org, info@weeksvillesociety.org | **Getting there** Subway to Utica Avenue (A, C, 3, 4) | **Hours** Tue–Thu 10am–5pm, tours at 3pm | **Tip** Visit the nearby site of the former Colored School No. 2, founded as the African School in 1839 (1634 Dean Street, Brooklyn, NY 11213). In 1893, the school merged with P.S. 83, becoming Brooklyn's first school to integrate students and teaching staff.

110 Woody Guthrie's Ashes
This land was his land – and final resting place

Just off the sand's edge at the end of the Coney Island boardwalk, a row of rocks jutting into the water marks the spot where legendary folk singer Woody Guthrie's family scattered his ashes following his death from Huntington's chorea in October 3, 1967. For several years, this stretch of the shoreline was the family playground to Woody, Marjorie, and their children. Marjorie's parents lived in Sea Gate, the gated residential community just beyond the jetty, while, for seven years, the Guthries lived a five-minute walk away in an apartment at 3520 Mermaid Avenue. That house no longer exists (it was torn down and replaced by a senior residential center), but while living there, Woody was at his most prolific creativity, writing classics like "1913 Massacre" and "Deportees," as well as children's and Hanukkah songs.

Gathering near the rocks, Marjorie used a beer can opener to poke a few holes in the green can containing his ashes, but when nothing would flow out, son Arlo ("Alice's Restaurant Massacree") climbed onto the rocks and heaved it into the sea. Afterwards, they walked to Nathan's (1310 Surf Avenue) for hot dogs and took a ride on the Wonder Wheel.

The Guthries also lived in another nearby location. With money earned from sales of The Weavers' recording of "So Long, It's Been Good to Know You," the family moved to 49 Murdock Court (#1J), part of the Beach Haven apartments developed by Fred C. Trump, father of Donald.

Unable to write musical notation because of his disease, Guthrie left behind hundreds of sets of completed lyrics for which no melodies exist. As a way of continuing her father's legacy, Nora Guthrie gave access to English folk singer Billy Bragg and American indie rockers Wilco, resulting in the award-winning album, "Mermaid Avenue." The home that appears on the album cover, similar to the Guthries' home, is at 2810 Mermaid Avenue.

Address The rocks near West 37th Street and Riegelmann Boardwalk, Brooklyn,
NY 11224 | Getting there Subway to Coney Island–Stillwell Avenue (D, F, N, Q), then
bus 36 to Surf Avenue–West 37th Street | Hours Unrestricted | Tip Wander down
Reigelmann's Boardwalk for a drink at the Parachute Bar at Kitchen 21 (3052 West 21st
Street, Brooklyn, NY 11224, www.kitchen-21.com), a rooftop bar at the former site of
Coney Island's historic Childs' Restaurant.

111__ The World of Tomorrow

Take a ride back to the future

The stairway down into the disused subway station that holds the New York Transit Museum offers no clue to the wonders that await there. Housing a collection that showcases everything from entry turnstiles and tokens to old subway maps and model trolley cars, nearly every aspect of the city's transit system is explored. Informative wall displays combine text and historic photos to tell the story of how a network that began with a ferry service between Manhattan and Brooklyn in 1642 morphed into a vast array of subways, trains, and buses that operates 24 hours a day, 7 days a week and is capable of transporting more than three billion riders annually.

Permanent exhibits provide the broad framework. Steel, Stone & Backbone explores the story of the laborers who built New York City's first underground system, approved for construction in 1894 and inaugurated in 1904. "On th Streets" takes a look at the evolution of the buses and trolleys that get us from here to there at street level. Speed of change is palpable, mimicking the city's tremendous growth. Electric trolleys arrived in Brooklyn only a decade after the arrival of the Brooklyn Bridge, energizing development of the borough's interior, until then still largely farmland. Vintage film footage allows you to experience a ride across the bridge (service began in 1898), moving at a whopping 8 mph. Meanwhile, a 12-seat city bus and "fish bowl" cab allow the kind of interactive access that kids will love.

Access is also a key component downstairs, where the museum maintains a display of vintage subway cars at the old station platform tracks. One, the BMT Q 1612C, has a particularly interesting history. A wooden elevated trolley car from 1908, it was repurposed as a cost-saving measure in 1939 to bring riders to the World's Fair – a thing of the past that transported attendees to "The World of Tomorrow."

Address Boerum Place and Schermerhorn Street, Brooklyn, NY 11201, +1 (718)694-1600, www.nytransitmuseum.org | **Getting there** Subway to Jay Street–Metrotech (A, F, R), or to Borough Hall (2, 3, 4, 5) | **Hours** Tue–Fri 10am–4pm, Sat & Sun 11am–5pm | **Tip** Visit the NY Transit Museum Annex Gallery & Store in Grand Central Terminal for miniature train exhibits and a store packed tight with MTA souvenirs and train memorabilia (89 East 42nd Street, New York, NY 10017, www.grandcentralterminal.com/shop/new-york-transit-museum-gallery-store).

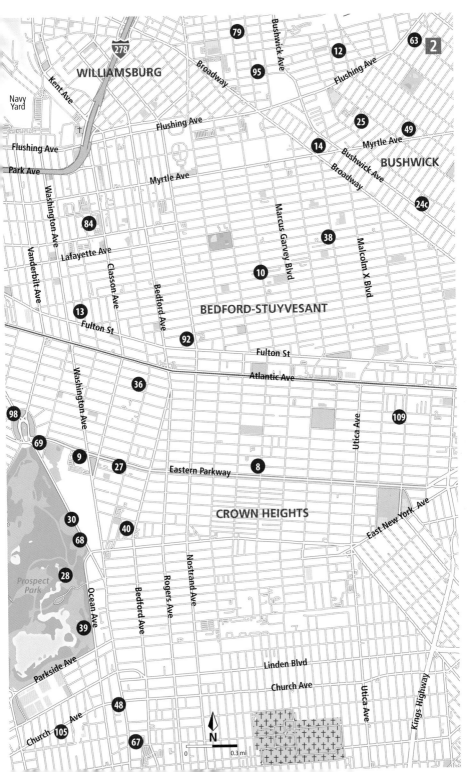

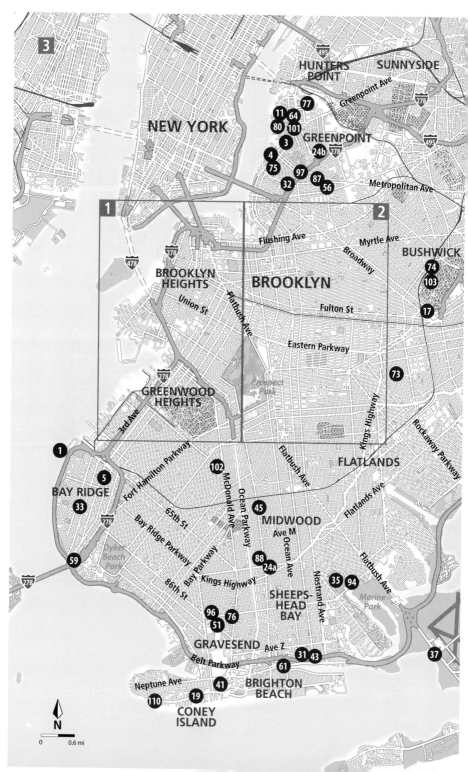

Wendy Lubovich, Ed Lefkowicz
**111 Museums in New York That
You Must Not Miss**
ISBN 978-3-7408-0379-7

Anita Mai Genua, Clare Davenport,
Elizabeth Lenell Davies
**111 Places in Toronto That You
Must Not Miss**
ISBN 978-3-7408-0257-8

Andréa Seiger
**111 Places in Washington D.C.
That You Must Not Miss**
ISBN 978-3-7408-0258-5

Elisabeth Larsen
**111 Places in The Twin Cities
That You Must Not Miss**
ISBN 978-3-7408-0029-1

Joe DiStefano, Clay Williams
**111 Places in Queens
That You Must Not Miss**
ISBN 978-3-7408-0020-8

Allison Robicelli, John Dean
**111 Places in Baltimore
That You Must Not Miss**
ISBN 978-3-7408-0158-8

Amy Bizzarri, Susie Inverso
**111 Places in Chicago
That You Must Not Miss**
ISBN 978-3-7408-0156-4

Laurel Moglen, Julia Posey,
Lyudmila Zotova
**111 Places in Los Angeles
That You Must Not Miss**
ISBN 978-3-95451-884-5

Gordon Streisand
**111 Places in Miami
and the Keys That
You Must Not Miss**
ISBN 978-3-95451-644-5

Floriana Petersen, Steve Werney
111 Places in San Francisco
That You Must Not Miss
ISBN 978-3-95451-609-4

Jo-Anne Elikann
111 Places in New York
That You Must Not Miss
ISBN 978-3-95451-052-8

Michael Murphy, Sally Asher
111 Places in New Orleans
That You Must Not Miss
ISBN 978-3-95451-645-2

Kathleen Becker
111 Places in Lisbon
That You Shouldn't Miss
ISBN 978-3-7408-0383-4

Alexia Amvrazi,
Diana Farr Louis, Diane Shugart
111 Places in Athens
That You Shouldn't Miss
ISBN 978-3-7408-0377-3

Alexandra Loske
111 Places in Brighton and
Lewes That You Shouldn't Miss
ISBN 978-3-7408-0255-4

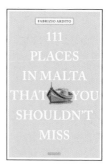

Fabrizio Ardito
111 Places in Malta
That You Shouldn't Miss
ISBN 978-3-7408-0261-5

Benjamin Haas, Leonie Friedrich
111 Places in Buenos Aires
That You Must Not Miss
ISBN 978-3-7408-0260-8

Beate C. Kirchner
111 Places in Rio de Janeiro
That You Must Not Miss
ISBN 978-3-7408-0262-2

Andrea Livnat,
Angelika Baumgartner
**111 Places in Tel Aviv
That You Shouldn't Miss**
ISBN 978-3-7408-0263-9

Kai Oidtmann
**111 Places in Iceland
That You Shouldn't Miss**
ISBN 978-3-7408-0030-7

Sybil Canac, Renée Grimaud,
Katia Thomas
**111 Places in Paris
That You Shouldn't Miss**
ISBN 978-3-7408-0159-5

Matěj Černý, Marie Peřinová
**111 Places in Prague
That You Shouldn't Miss**
ISBN 978-3-7408-0144-1

Beate C. Kirchner
**111 Places in Florence
and Northern Tuscany
That You Must Not Miss**
ISBN 978-3-95451-613-1

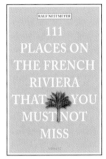

Ralf Nestmeyer
**111 Places on the French
Riviera That You Must
Not Miss**
ISBN 978-3-95451-612-4

Giulia Castelli Gattinara,
Mario Verin
**111 Places in Milan
That You Must Not Miss**
ISBN 978-3-95451-331-4

Petra Sophia Zimmermann
**111 Places in Verona and Lake
Garda That You Must Not Miss**
ISBN 978-3-95451-611-7

Marcus X. Schmid
**111 Places in Istanbul
That You Must Not Miss**
ISBN 978-3-95451-423-6

Annett Klingner
111 Places in Rome
That You Must Not Miss
ISBN 978-3-95451-469-4

Ralf Nestmeyer
111 Places in Provence
That You Must Not Miss
ISBN 978-3-95451-422-9

Rüdiger Liedtke
111 Places on Mallorca
That You Shouldn't Miss
ISBN 978-3-95451-281-2

Tom Shields, Gillian Tait
111 Places in Glasgow
That You Shouldn't Miss
ISBN 978-3-7408-0256-1

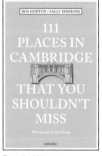

Rosalind Horton,
Sally Simmons, Guy Snape
111 Places in Cambridge
That You Shouldn't Miss
ISBN 978-3-7408-0147-2

Justin Postlethwaite
111 Places in Bath
That You Shouldn't Miss
ISBN 978-3-7408-0146-5

Gillian Tait
111 Places in Edinburgh
That You Shouldn't Miss
ISBN 978-3-95451-883-8

Julian Treuherz,
Peter de Figueiredo
111 Places in Liverpool
That You Shouldn't Miss
ISBN 978-3-95451-769-5

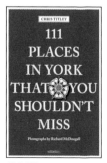

Chris Titley
111 Places in York
That You Shouldn't Miss
ISBN 978-3-95451-768-8

Acknowledgements

I'd like to thank my editor, Karen Seiger, for her immense patience, support, and friendship throughout this process. Many thanks to Ed Lefkowicz for his beautiful images of these 111 places. My thanks, too, to Katie Boswell who very ably assisted me with research. Many friends made wonderful suggestions and offered support, especially Karen Plafker and Brian Horace. Both were appreciated in equal measure. This work is dedicated to the people who matter most – my wonderful family, including my children Chelsea, Dylan, and Rosalind, and, especially, my loving partner Deb Schultz, who has supported me throughout. A native and lifelong resident of Brooklyn, she gave generously from the fount of her vast knowledge of this borough we love.

– John Major

My most profuse thanks to my wife Cynthia Lefkowicz for her forbearance and encouragement throughout the length of this project, and for suggesting and orchestrating our move from New England to Brooklyn over 7 years ago. If cities are where ideas go to have sex, this city is arguably the most fertile, and my creative life is greatly improved for being part of it. To Karen Seiger I owe much for bringing me into this project, and to John Major for his words and insight. Finally, thanks to the memory of my father Constanty Lefkowicz, who first introduced me to the magic of photography.

– Ed Lefkowicz

The author

John Major writes about art and culture, especially events and places in Brooklyn, his home for the last 12 years. He is also writing a memoir about life as a stay-at-home father of three managing a divorce and international relocation, uniquely told through pilgrimages to paintings by the Italian artist, Caravaggio. Originally from southern Ohio, John is a dedicated explorer of cities. Among his favorites are London (which he called home for a dozen years), Barcelona, Rome, and Paris. He is determined to never lose the sense of wonder from being a curious explorer, both at home and abroad.

The photographer

Ed Lefkowicz is a commercial, corporate, and editorial photographer. A native New Englander who eventually moved to Brooklyn with his wife Cynthia, he enjoys exploring New York City life in all its storied quirkiness. Never without a camera, he chronicles the cognitive dissonances that color life in the boroughs with his alt website TheQuirkySide.com. As photo editor of *Edible Queens* magazine, he fancies himself a saveur and may have been the first to introduce the American term "foodie" to to the French.